How to Kill the Job Culture Before it Kills You

Living a Life of Autonomy in a Wage-Slave Society

by Claire Wolfe

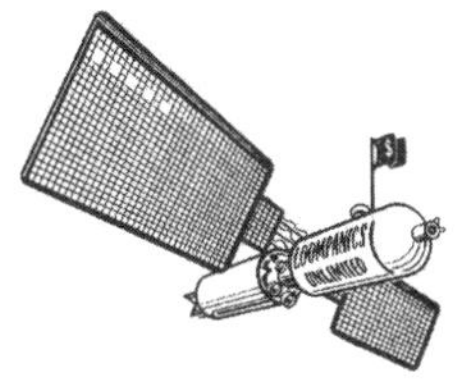

Loompanics Unlimited
Port Townsend, Washington

How to Kill the Job Culture Before it Kills You
Living a Life of Autonomy in a Wage-Slave Society

Published by:
Loompanics Unlimited
PO Box 1197
Port Townsend, WA 98368
Loompanics Unlimited is a division of Loompanics Enterprises, Inc.
Phone: 360-385-2230
Fax: 360-385-7785
E-mail: service@loompanics.com
Web site: www.loompanics.com

Cover art by Craig Howell, Cheeba Productions

ISBN 1-55950247-9
Library of Congress Card Catalog Number 2005930175

But yield who will to their separation,
My object in living is to unite
My avocation with my vocation
As my two eyes make one in sight.
Only where love and need are one
And the work is play for mortal stakes
Is the deed ever really done
For Heaven and the future's sakes.
— Robert Frost, "*Two Tramps in Mud Time*"

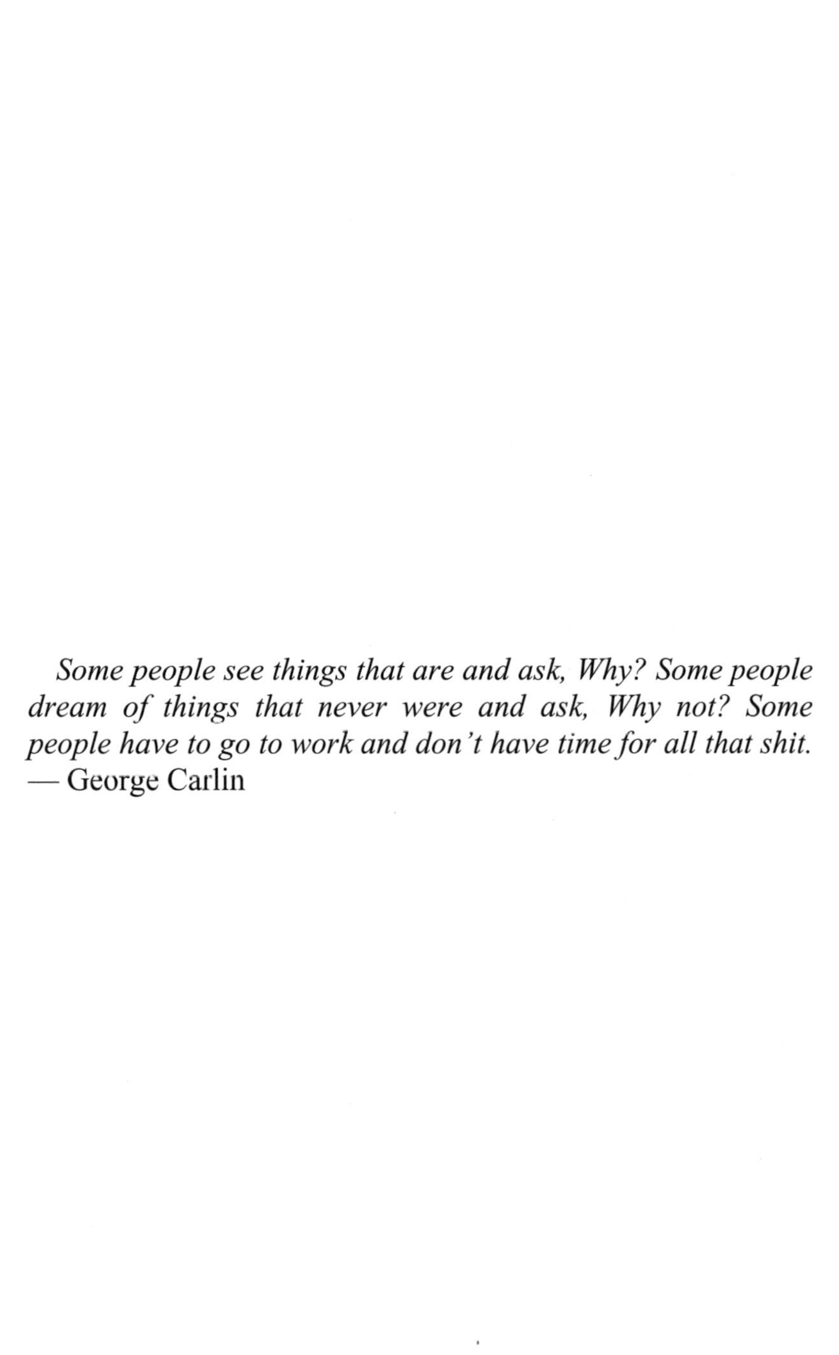

Some people see things that are and ask, Why? Some people dream of things that never were and ask, Why not? Some people have to go to work and don't have time for all that shit.
— George Carlin

Contents

This Book Aims to Do Two Things 1
Good Work in a Good Life 3
Introduction:
Jobs Suck (The Vitality Out of Life) 5

Part I: Why Jobs Suck

Chapter One:
Inventing the Job Culture 17
Chapter Two:
The Classic Case Against Jobs 33
Chapter Three:
The Free-Market Case Against Jobs 41

Part II: Freeing Ourselves

Chapter Four:
Getting a Goal 59
Chapter Five:
Workstyle Options 75
Chapter Six:
Practical Steps 95

Part III: The Rest of the World

Chapter Seven:
The Jobless Future 123
Chapter Eight:
Getting There 139

Acknowledgements

Special thanks to Liberty Lightning who reminded me about Frost's "Two Tramps in Mud Time;" to Gia Cosindas, editor extraordinaire, who brainstormed me through a tough patch in the writing; and to Keith Perkins for permission to use his poem "Gone Croatoan." Thanks as always to Mike, Audrey, Jan, and the rest of the Loompanics crew, with special kudos to the world's most accurate and speedy shipping department.

Quotes used throughout this book came from many sources, but especially from:

Appaloosa Business Services (www.spottedhorse.com/);

Cool Funny Jokes (www.coolfunnyjokes.com);

Famous Quotes (home.att.net/~quotations/index.html); and Wisdom Quotes (www.wisdomquotes.com).

This Book Aims to Do Two Things

The first is to help anyone who wants to break out of the job trap and into a more independent, "organic," self-chosen, satisfying way of living — in which your work serves your life, rather than your life being something you squeeze into spare time after an exhausting work day.

The second aim is to question — and hopefully someday replace — the whole Job Culture. The Job Culture (which we'll define shortly) is a comprehensive and unnatural way of life that permeates nearly everything we do. The Job Culture has become so ingrained in modern society that we're hardly even aware that such a parasite has attached itself to us. We consider it simply "the way things are." Yet it's sapping the vitality out of our lives, families, and communities.

The book's first aim is eminently do-able for most people. It's simply a matter of whether we want to achieve it enough to make the effort.

The second aim is more abstract, speculative, and possibly even absurdly idealistic. I can only hope this little tome will get a few thousand people thinking in a creative direction that could result in long-term change.

The change is desperately needed.

We will not fully recapture our lives and liberties until we've stamped out the assumption that it's normal to separate our work lives completely from our home, family, and community lives. Normal to subject ourselves to rigid schedules even when they're unnecessary. Normal to obey arbitrary rules even when some other procedure makes more sense. Normal to cram and squeeze the entire rest of our lives around the single act of making money — when making money ought to be simply the act that supports the more personal, more important, more gratifying, parts of our lives.

The very fact that such patent abnormalities have become an accepted part of the fabric of most people's lives is a prime sign of how desperately we need change.

Good Work in a Good Life

This book is about the process of seeking a life — and eventually a culture — in which work, family, community, and personal interests can be more healthfully blended. It is about finding personal satisfaction in the act of earning a living. It is about *balance*. About *seeking* that balance. It is about wresting control of our own lives back from institutionalized systems — hopefully without giving up the best benefits those systems have brought us.

It's not about bashing anyone's particular job or life.

Even before finishing the book, I began to hear from people protesting that they had jobs they absolutely loved that supported lifestyles they enjoyed. Good on you. If you love both your job and your life, you may have already achieved your perfect balance. If anybody has a problem with that, tell 'em to go stuff it.

It is possible to have a good job — one that sustains and fits within a good, enjoyable life. But it is not possible to have a healthy *Job Culture*. And it is not healthy to structure an entire life around the mere act of earning money.

So for the millions who are unsatisfied with their own work, and for the millions who try to live a good, balanced, centered life while uneasily surrounded by a frenzied culture of compulsion and consumption — this book is about *options.*

> *The more I want to get something done, the less I call it work.* — Richard Bach

Introduction
Jobs Suck
(The Vitality Out of Life)

Modern-day men and women have come to serve the machine — that is, to work at a fixed job, usually at fixed hours, for a business we don't own, in conditions not of our own making. We do this to create products or deliver services over which we have little input or control.

As employees, we usually receive a fixed wage for our efforts. If our work produces an unusually good result, the benefit of that return goes largely to others — quitc often to faraway others whose names we don't even know.

If we produce some astonishing innovation or perform at consistently high levels, we may also receive a bonus or a promotion. On the other hand, we may actually be punished for performance above the call of duty (for instance, when we fail to confine ourselves to what our union demands, or when our co-workers perceive our extra labors or innovations as a form of brown-nosing).

There's a disconnect between what we do and the reward we receive.

Worse, there's a disconnect between what we do and our responsibility for our own actions. We may work for an institution whose products are harmful or whose practices are corrupt and predatory; but we shrug and tell ourselves it's not our fault. *We're just the little guys; we have no power to change what the big guys do.*

Some of us may also get paid for wasting our own time in meaningless labor; but we shrug and say, "Well, it's a living."

> *It's just a job. Grass grows, birds fly, waves pound the sand. I beat people up.* — Muhammad Ali

Today, more and more of us work as tax-paid bureaucrats or enforcers of laws, rules, and regulations. When we do that, we produce nothing. We simply keep the machinery of the Job Culture running — enforcing its demands and reinforcing its complexities.

Even if we love our work, produce something of value, and labor for an employer who honors and cherishes us, we often hate the arbitrary restrictions and hassles that go with our jobs. Think: time clocks, daily commutes, suits, pantyhose, gray cubicles, PC speech restrictions, gossiping co-workers, pressuring bosses, bureaucratic paperwork, huge chunks of money taken out of our paychecks before we ever see them, privacy invasions, non-sensical rules, pointless meetings, exhaustion, screaming telephones, other constant interruptions, unsafe or uncomfortable working conditions, traffic, indigestion-inducing lunches, high taxes, *ad infinitum*.

> *A generation ago Americans believed that their working hours would decline, their leisure increase, and their real incomes soar. As it has turned out, none of these expectations proved accurate. ...Americans today work more, shop for longer hours, and have less leisure time than they did in the 1960s.* — Prof. David Nye

Nevertheless, serving the machine has undeniably made us more prosperous than our agrarian ancestors. It has enabled us to amass more possessions, live in larger houses, have more sophisticated health care, live longer, and enjoy many other benefits.

It's also true that this frantic and fragmented Job Culture we live in, and these frantic and fragmented jobs millions of us hold, are in many ways *necessary* to a complex, modern world. We cannot craft microprocessors in quaint Amish workshops. We cannot splice genes at our kitchen table. We cannot mass-produce vehicles in the village smithy. We cannot make millions of cheap watches, wearables, or widgets without automated mass-production.

And oh my, do we ever love our widgets. And our clean, bright stores. And our increased product safety. And improved sanitation. And many other genuine benefits of today's life.

So we tell ourselves we're better off than those ancestors with their crude village shops, their poor communications, their limited and costly goods, their frighteningly primitive medicine, and their city streets running with sewage.

Then we wonder why we're not happy.

Even if our belief in the benefits of serving the industrial or post-industrial machine is justified, we're still paying a terrible cost. Millions of us drag ourselves to jobs we hate. We can't be with our families when they need us. Our communities increasingly lack cohesion. Our children are raised and schooled by paid strangers who usually represent bureaucratic interests more than our own.

We force ourselves to perform endless, repetitive tasks for the sake of money, even when our body and our mind are both screaming that we should be resting or doing some more personally satisfying work. We suffer anomie, exhaustion, and a hundred physical and mental syndromes, from carpal tunnel and fibromyalgia to chronic depression.

We medicate ourselves. We spend hours with our mental-health counselors. We desperately seek after-hours diversion in television, video games, drinking, shopping, and other mindless activities. And we trudge onward.

We must stop taking all our miseries for granted! We should stop being satisfied with our dissatisfaction. We need to ask ourselves: Isn't there a better way to live? A way that will enable us to be prosperous without robbing us of our health, our families, and our connection to our selves?

Work vs. Jobs

There is a difference between work — which human beings need for survival and contentment — and jobs. Jobs as we now know them are a recent innovation. An innovation imposed upon millions by economic forces beyond our control. An innovation that has been more destructive to us — and to the world around us — than we like to admit.

Every job requires work (even if it's only the work of trying to look busy while doing nothing or the work of spinning our wheels on useless tasks). But every form of productive work doesn't necessarily require a job.

> *Most people work just hard enough not to get fired and get paid just enough money not to quit.* — George Carlin

Most of the human race existed for millennia without jobs as we know them today, but with work that was sometimes indistinguishable from play and that was more varied than much of the work we do today.

The job — with its arbitrary rules, dislocations, repetitions, monotony, and rigid structures — is in many cases a sort of parasite, clinging to, but not aiding, the useful work. The job saps energy that could better be used for other purposes. Not only that; in many cases the job parasite attached to the useful work could have died 50 or 100 years ago and not been missed by anybody. Instead it survives because we tolerate it and continue to keep it alive with our own sweat and blood. And because we accept that the way things are now is just "the way it is."

One aim of this book is for us to be able to have useful, interesting work while freeing ourselves as much as possible from the worst ugliness of the job world.

When I talk about "freeing ourselves," I'm not merely talking about self-employment, volunteer work, or the work of being a house-spouse and parent — all familiar forms of jobless employment. I'm talking about earning-a-living work that can be done without artificial conditions imposed by outside forces. Work that's naturally integrated into family and community life. Work that lets us be there for our children and partners when they need us — and allows them to be there for us. Work that enables us to carve out time for our other interests. Work that enables us to carve out time to think and to relax. Or work that we love so much that we happily do it without having to enclose it — and ourselves! — within artificial structures designed to meet institutional needs more than our own.

Work and Jobs vs. the Job Culture

Just as there is a difference between a job and work, there's also a distinction between our personal work (whatever it may be) and the Job Culture within which we work.

Today, whether we have a job, independent work, or no work at all, nearly all of us in the western world (and increasingly in the developing world, too) live under the benign tyranny of the Job Culture.

How to Kill the Job Culture Before it Kills You

10

The Job Culture is that entire portion of our lives and our society that is dominated and shaped by institutionalized work systems. It extends far beyond work itself. The Job Culture includes not only the office or the factory and all that takes place there. It includes the attitudes, activities, and institutions we've developed in society to help us cope with a world in which job-holding is the major daily occupation of the adult population (and in which job-like institutionalized schooling occupies our children).

Here are a few examples of what I mean:

- We gobble fast food after a long day at the office (and feed it to our children) not because we really like the stuff or think it's the best for growing bodies, but simply because we're too tired to prepare something better. The growth of a global, multi-billion dollar industrialized fast-food industry is a manifestation of the Job Culture.
- We pay taxes at a level that would have shocked our great-grandparents, simply because the money is taken out of our paychecks in such small increments that we're unaware of the magnitude of the seizure. (We may even rejoice at getting "free money" back after filing our 1040s, not considering that it's simply our own money returning to us after being loaned, interest-free to the government.) High taxes, paid without angry protest, are a price of living in the Job Culture.
- We want to go to the beach for the weekend, but we can't leave when it's convenient for us because all those job-holders have the roads jammed solid during the hours we'd like to travel. Traffic jams — and for that matter, our periodic and highly scheduled rushes toward "recreation" — are both products of the Job Culture.

- We pay high health-insurance costs not just because of our aging population or advances in medical technology (as the media tell us); but because employer-paid insurance has created both a giant bureaucracy and a disconnect between the customers of health care (us) and the institutions who pay the bills (corporations and tax-funded bureaucracies). Hidden — and rising — costs to sustain institutional health-care bureaucracies are a natural result of the Job Culture.
- Bureaucrats increasingly provide services once performed by local volunteer efforts and community self-help. Taken over by professionals (for whom it's just a job), "human services" become increasingly expensive, impersonal, depersonalizing, and regimented. Depersonalization, bureaucracy, and all that go with them are direct outgrowths of the Job Culture.
- We live among neighbors who are increasingly inert and dependent on far-off bureaucratic (corporate or government) institutions for their sustenance. Passive dependence and community fragmentation follow the Job Culture as night follows day.

Smash it

Millions of us have lost the connection between the work we do and the larger life in which that work belongs. Living in the Job Culture, we dwell among millions who suffer the same disconnect, but are not even aware of what's happening to them — and to us.

They accept as normal a way of life that is profoundly abnormal and unhealthy. Even when they perceive the social problems of the Job Culture, they accept the word of bureaucrats and politicians that top-down, institutionalized solutions — Job Culture solutions — can solve those problems. So we become buried in ever-deeper layers of centralization, bureaucratization, and de-personalization. We're in a vicious circle because we go on believing that each new problem will be solved by the very same methods that created it.

But millions don't even think or care about underlying causes of our cultural disaffection. They're too busy rushing unreflectively, desperately through life. Forget fruitless, bureaucratic solutions to cultural problems. They hope the fanciest car, the best clothes, the coolest vacation, or the latest trendy gadget will bring them personal happiness. And so they go deeply into debt, guaranteeing their own desperate long-term need to work longer and harder. Then they wonder why happiness eludes them.

This book is a modest proposal for helping individuals free themselves and for (ultimately) replacing the Job Culture with a one in which individuals are both more independent and (this is no contradiction) more inter-dependent. That is, a culture in which individuals value themselves and their autonomy so highly they won't sell such a large portion of their lives to institutions; but also a culture in which we recognize that the independent individuals around us are ultimately far more vital to our well-being than far-off bureaucrats or the executives of any Mega-Global Corp, Inc.

What this book isn't

There are also some things this book is definitely *not.*

It is not a proposal for restoring some mythical, pre-industrial Eden. It is not a proposal for doing away with modern culture. It is not a rejection of technology.

It is not a proposal for *political* change. No amount of lobbying, legislation, regulation, or *force majeure* can produce a healthy culture in which work, family, community, and leisure exist in organic wholeness. Producing a healthy culture is up to us, as individuals, families, friends and neighbors.

This book is ...

...a proposal for changing the world by changing ourselves. Whether or not we can effect major change in the world, we definitely can change our own lives for the better.

At the very least, by changing our own perceptions and patterns, we create more personal contentment. And we relate differently to the existing world. At most, we begin a ripple-in-the-pond change that influences the world around us to become a happier, more sustaining place.

If you're content with your own work life and with the Job Culture you see around you, then this isn't the book for you. But if you've wondered what's wrong and what to do about it, read on.

In Part I, we'll examine how we got into the job trap and the Job Culture and look at some of the historic and modern objections to this way of living.

In Part II, we'll get down to the nitty gritty of how to extricate ourselves from the job trap — or how to make our jobs less of a trap for us personally.

Then, in the brief Part III, we'll take a look at how we might ultimately heal the wounds the Job Culture has inflicted on our societies and we'll examine what a healthier society might be like.

Part I:
Why Jobs Suck

Taking into account getting ready for work, commuting to work, talking about our jobs, and worrying about getting laid off, we will have spent more time during our working lives thinking about work than thinking about all our other concerns in life. — Ernie J. Zelinski[1]

[1] Zelinski, Ernie J. *The Joy of Not Working*. Ten Speed Press, Berkeley, CA, 1997. p. 4.

Chapter One
Inventing the Job Culture

There never was an Eden.

Before ordinary people became enslaved to the clock, the wage, the factory, the silver chains of "benefits," and the Job Culture, they were enslaved, in one way or another, to popes, kings, local lordlings, merchant guilds, or other powers. They usually lived in squalor and often died young. They were at the mercy of the weather and the quality of the land they had to farm. A bad harvest or a long winter could mean hunger.

They were indeed worse off than we in many, many ways. Anyone who hopes to see the entire world chuck off modernity and go back to some phantasmal paradise of the past (as some neo-primitivists, neo-paleoliths, or just-plain-Luddites do) is playing a dangerous game.

That said, however, when the Industrial Revolution came roaring over the landscape of England, America, and other countries of the West, it swept away much that was good and brought with it much that was terrible. Consequences, both good and abysmal, remain with us to this day.

What exactly was the Industrial Revolution, though? Here's the bare-bones encyclopedia version of the story:

> **Industrial Revolution:** Widespread replacement of manual labor by machines that began in Britain in the 18th century and is still continuing in some parts of the world. The Industrial Revolution was the result of many fundamental, interrelated changes that transformed agricultural economies into industrial ones. The most immediate changes were in the nature of production: what was produced, as well as where and how. Goods that had traditionally been made in the home or in small workshops began to be manufactured in the factory. Productivity and technical efficiency grew dramatically, in part through the systematic application of scientific and practical knowledge to the manufacturing process. Efficiency was also enhanced when large groups of business enterprises were located within a limited area. The Industrial Revolution led to the growth of cities as people moved from rural areas into urban communities in search of work.
>
> The changes brought by the Industrial Revolution overturned not only traditional economies, but also whole societies. Economic changes caused far-reaching social changes, including the movement of people to cities, the availability of a greater variety of material goods, and new ways of doing business. The Industrial Revolution was the first step in modern economic growth and development. Economic development was combined with superior military technology to make the nations of Europe and their cultural offshoots, such as the United States, the most powerful in the world in the 18th and 19th centuries.[1]

True, as far as it goes. Actually, the move toward manufacturing with mechanized devices had been building since the

---

1 http://encarta.msn.com/encyclopedia_761577952/Industrial_Revolution.html

Middle Ages. But the real *culture* of the machine age — the Job Culture — didn't begin to take hold until around 1760.

Prior to that, the economy of the western world was based on farming, herding, handcrafting, and small-scale enterprise. (In fact, the very notion of "the economy" as a monolithic thing is itself the product of the centrally controlled, top-down thinking that came in with the Industrial Revolution.)

Before the Industrial Revolution, machines largely helped skilled individuals perform manual tasks more effectively. After the revolution, unskilled or semi-skilled individuals essentially became servants to factory machines, and many skilled workers were supplanted, their life skills rendered obsolete.

Although some rural dwellers were driven into factories against their will as their grazing lands were enclosed and their handcrafting work became uncompetitive, many younger people no doubt embraced factory jobs as an escape from domestic drudgery and the stultifying life of farmsteads, villages, and towns. Millions certainly enjoyed, and continue to enjoy, the cheap, plentiful goods the new Job Culture produced.

The World is Too Much With Us

The World is too much with us; late and soon,
Getting and spending, we lay waste our powers:
Little we see in Nature that is ours;
We have given our hearts away, a sordid boon!
This Sea that bares her bosom to the moon,
The winds that will be howling at all hours
And are up-gather'd now like sleeping flowers,
For this, for everything, we are out of tune;
It moves us not.-Great God! I'd rather be
A pagan suckled in a creed outworn,-
So might I, standing on this pleasant lea,
Have glimpses that would make me less forlorn;

Have sight of Proteus rising from the sea;
Or hear old Triton blow his wreathèd horn.
— William Wordsworth, 1807

Mixed blessing, mixed curse

The Industrial Revolution was neither the great evil that neo-primitivists and some environmentalists think it was nor the unalloyed holy blessing generations of American school children were taught that it was.

Like most other human endeavors, industrialization brought a mixed bag of blessings and curses.

No doubt many mill builders or machinery inventors saw their work as a profound benefit to society, as well as a great boon to their own pocketbooks. But from the beginning, the bad and good came down together on an unsuspecting, and often uncomprehending, populace.

Take one fairly typical example of the unintended consequences of mechanization: The invention of the cotton gin. When Eli Whitney created a mechanical means of separating cotton seeds from useful fiber in 1793, it gave a tremendous boost to textile manufacturing. The textile industry had been among the first to automate. Only the lack of a rapid de-seeding process prevented an enormous increase in low-cost production of cotton fabric.

The cotton gin made it possible to process cotton balls into useful fiber up to 50 times faster than with previous manual or crude mechanical methods. What happened next was awesome:

> The year before that invention the United States exported less than one hundred and forty thousand pounds of cotton; the year after it, nearly half a million pounds; the next year over a million and a half; a year later still, over six million; by 1800, nearly eighteen million pounds a year. And by 1845

> the United States was producing seven-eighths of the world's cotton.[2]

Cotton, previously a minor, uneconomical crop, became "king" in the South.

But the cotton gin was no boon to the slaves who had to pick the cotton.

By 1793, slavery was rapidly dying in the United States. The reasons were both moral and economic.

The moral reasons: Following the War of Independence, Americans were increasingly aware that the equal rights they'd fought for weren't being applied equally. People of conscience realized that was a terrible injustice.

The economic: Many planters had more laborers than they could use and were considering emancipating their slaves. It simply didn't make sense to go on housing and feeding unneeded workers.

But all that changed with the cotton gin. Suddenly, with rapid, inexpensive cotton processing available, the South was covered in vast tracts of an extremely labor-intensive crop. Cheap labor was needed to pick all that new cotton. Slaves' work days lengthened. The overseer's lash drove men, women, and children ever harder — all to serve the machine and the market for cotton cloth.

But that wasn't even the worst for the poor slaves. The moral reasons for abolishing slavery remained, even if the economic reasons had been derailed. So just 14 years after the invention of the cotton gin, conscience-stricken humanitarians succeeded in passing a law that forbade importation of any more slaves to the United States. Another unintended consequence then struck.

---

2 Thompson, Holland. "Eli Whitney and the Cotton Gin." From *The Age of Invention: A Chronicle of Mechanical Conquest.* 1921. http://inventors.about.com/cs/inventorsalphabet/a/cotton_gin_2.htm

As a result of this "humane" law, the existing slaves were forced to bear an ever-larger work burden because no other workers could legally be hauled over from Africa.

> *If a man does only what is required of him, he is a slave. If a man does more than is required of him, he is a free man.* — Chinese Proverb

The increasing cruelty of labor and the desperate plight of overworked slaves led to rebellions, including the famous and bloody uprising led by Nat Turner in 1831. White Quakers, free blacks, and people of conscience in the North became increasingly convinced that slavery must end soon ... and this time, instead of moving toward a gradual, peaceful demise, slavery was ended only after the most violent, bloody conflict Americans have ever endured.

So the wondrous cotton gin, pride of the Industrial Revolution, led to cheaper cloth, but also to more human misery. And it ultimately became one of numerous factors leading to the War Between the States.

One could spend a lifetime cataloging such chains of consequence throughout the Industrial Revolution. Even the dispassionate *Encarta* entry above gives yet another example of the horrors that have come with the benefits of the Industrial Revolution: Increasing technology made possible increasingly sophisticated, impersonal warmaking. And goes on doing so to this day.

Other examples: fast, affordable computers have opened an entirely new world of productivity and communication. At the same time, they've actually *hindered* our productivity in many ways (e.g. by forcing us to spend endless time upgrading, maintaining, and troubleshooting them; by offering various new distractions; and by forcing us to spend endless hours on business-related e-mails). Computers have also enabled unprecedented spying and tracking of our activities by both commercial and government snoops. In the mid 1990s, computer enthusiasts (including me) exulted that the Internet was an unstoppable tool for achieving freedom. Ten years later, even the greatest tech-boosters had to admit that web bugs, userids, keystroke loggers, vast easily searchable databases, and other Internet-delivered "features" could be tools of tyrannical control.

Similarly, radio-frequency ID chips (RFID) show promise of being excellent inventory-tracking tools for cost-conscious global businesses — not to mention a boon to anybody who loves and loses a wandering pet. The tiny, implantable chips, however, also threaten to become a tool of "human inventory" tracking. Implanted ID chips will — this is a virtual certainty — ultimately control whether we are permitted to enter our workplace, get money from an ATM, drive on the highways, and eventually even whether or not we'll be "allowed" to buy groceries. Even in a less draconian and futuristic scenario, RFID chips will, within a few years, be attached to products we buy and will sometimes identify us and our habits to complete strangers. Walk into one store carrying a bag of merchandise from another store and conceivably the new store could read all your purchases. Couple that with your credit card information and they have a profile on you that they can use or sell. Even worse: If you sell a car that has old tires on it, and if the new owner dumps those tires illegally, the RFID chips (that the government is even now planning to require) in the tires tell the EPA that you're responsible for the pollution.

Another example: Modern, mass-produced firearms are truly "the great equalizer." They enable the weak to defend themselves against the strong in unprecedented ways. "Damsels" no longer have to hope for pre-industrial knights to rescue them; they can blow marauders away by firing a controlled pair of rounds from their own Glock or Ruger. Oppressed people can fight back against tyrants. But modern, mass-produced firearms (and the even more sophisticated weapons that have grown from firearms technology) also enable governments to commit war on an unprecedented scale. When governments manage to corner the market on effective weaponry, they can also use these tools to oppress and slaughter their own subjects far more effectively than tyrants of 2,000 years ago could. And of course, in the hands of freelance criminals and careless fools, guns can wreak havoc.

Computers, RFID chips, and firearms are all products, benefits, and potentially drawbacks of industrialization. Computers and firearms have potential to increase human freedom, but also have potential to oppress.

> *Everything that is really great and inspiring is created by the individual who can labor in freedom.* — Albert Einstein

We must always keep in mind that, whether we're talking about improving the world via the Industrial Revolution or improving the world by doing away with some of that revolution's after effects, we're talking about a tricky mix of benefits and drawbacks, neither hell nor Eden. But since we have been taught so relentlessly to value the benefits of rapid production of affordable products, it's well past time that all of us should consider the real price of those goods and those industrial methods, as well.

The growth of the Job Culture

Encarta makes a common — but not quite accurate — statement. It says the Industrial Revolution resulted in "widespread replacement of manual labor by machines." If that were true, people would have had to labor less, not more, as the factories multiplied across the landscape.

Not only that, but we'd be taking it even easier in these post-industrial days. And frankly, I haven't noticed a whole heck of a lot of leisure going on, have you?

> *[T]he early Europeans didn't have a term for work as we know it today. Although European peasants in the Middle Ages were poor and oppressed, they didn't work long hours. They celebrated holidays in the honor of even the most obscure saints; consequently, with time, they had more holidays and fewer and fewer workdays. The normal number of holidays at one time was 115 a year. Then along came the work ethic...* — Ernie J. Zelinski

What really happened is that slow, but *skilled* manual labor was largely replaced by unskilled or semi-skilled manual labor — the labor of tending machines or shifting machine-made products from one location to another. Interesting work was replaced by dull routine. Work done in the open air was replaced by labor performed in dark, roaring, hellish factories. Work that exercised the entire body was (and is) increasingly replaced by repetitious and/or sedentary tasks that taxed the body year after year in ways for which it was never designed. Work done at the workers' own pace was replaced by rigid scheduling. By bells. By clocks. By mottos like "If you don't come to work on Sunday, don't come to work on Monday."

The Job Culture had begun. Here are just a few of the specific changes that new, foreign, machine-driven culture imposed:

- Factory workers were forced to toil long, fixed hours, taking breaks only when authority figures allowed them to. They even learned to regulate their bladders and bowels according to supervisors' orders.

- Clocks and bells replaced seasons, tasks, and personal needs as the drivers of the work day and the work year.
- Workers were forced to neglect family members. Husbands and wives could no longer work side by side (as they had on farms or in workshops). Mothers working in factories could no longer tend their infants and children. The breakup of the family had begun, and continues to this day.
- Because the factory worker came to rely on a paycheck provided by a remote employer, home-based and community-based manufacturing businesses began to disappear, and communities themselves began to fragment as their citizens had less and less stake in them.
- Because factories benefited by centralization, rural communities began to die as cities grew.
- Profits — once largely earned and spent within the community — began to go to ever-more-distant business owners. Only wages (and in some cases, the cost of some supplies) — a mere fraction of the overall economic benefit of any workplace — remained to be spent on the worker's home ground.
- Compulsory, highly regimented government schooling replaced more individualized schooling. The explicit purpose of such schooling was not to educate independent individuals, but to homogenize the populace into being obedient soldiers, efficient bureaucrats, and willing factory workers. Compulsory, mass-production schooling also eventually became the Industrial Revolution's "solution" to the Industrial-Revolution-caused problem of children laboring long hours in factories.
- Conformity and cooperation became more valued than individual effort.

- Large, centralized welfare organizations (first private, later governmental) began to grow up to try to fix a variety of Industrial Revolution-caused social catastrophes: neglected children, orphaned children, unemployed workers, foul slums, etc. In other words, problems that either hadn't existed at all or that had been solved through community or extended-family self-help, generated permanent, institutional, and impersonal "solutions" that often only made matters worse for those on the receiving end of the "help." These top-down organizations also created permanent bureaucratic classes whose own economic well-being relied on an everlasting supply of needy, dependent "victims."
- People who had formerly provided for themselves and been more-or-less ignored by the wealthy now learned to accept being patronized by the powerful. The average man or woman (once relatively independent and inter-dependent) were exploited by some for their labors, "protected" by others for their helplessness, and treated as an "asset" or "resource" by yet others — to be valued for specific functions, but not to be valued as an independent and equal citizen.

Does any of the above sound familiar? Aren't our lives and our societies today run upon some variation of all the above?

> *One machine can do the work of fifty ordinary men.*
> *No machine can do the work of one extraordinary man.*
> — Elbert Hubbard

The Industrial Revolution began a process that has been crucial to our economic enjoyment, but that has also left us with today's terrible — and worsening — disconnect between what we do and who we are as individuals and as social beings.

Most of us no longer have an intimate connection to the earth or its seasons (for good or ill). Most of us no longer have an intimate connection with the products of our own labors. Most of us no longer live in families or communities where our labor and the rest of our lives are organically linked. Most of us no longer have the satisfaction of making something in which we can take personal pride. Most of us are no longer independent individuals, but cogs in a business or governmental system.

If our factory-slave ancestors had to work under more grim conditions than we do, at least they had enough self-respect not to pee in a bottle for their employers or permit their privacy to be raped via a background check or a prying psychological evaluation. They may have suffered cruel supervisors who lurked behind the machinery to make sure they didn't talk too much or take too many breaks. But they didn't have employers who monitored every second of their communications, trained cameras on their every movement, or demanded their fingerprints, iris-prints, or DNA as a job condition. Nobody forced our ancestors to submit to radio-frequency ID chips or voracious databases as a basic condition of living and working.

So we believe we're better off? But we can go on believing that only as long as we point selectively at the benefits while ignoring the increasing dehumanization, regimentation, homogenization, and surveillance being imposed on us. Degrading, patronizing, distrusting Big Brotherism has become so much a part of our lives that most of us neglect even to get angry about it — as genuinely independent, self-determining individuals would.

Ancient Greeks thought work was vulgar. Work, just for the sake of work, signified slavery and a lack of productivity. The only reason for work was to acquire more

> *leisure. Socrates stated that because manual laborers had no time for friendship or for serving the community, they made bad citizens and undesirable friends. The early Greeks and the Romans relegated all activities done with the hands, done under orders, or done for wages to the lower-class citizens or to the slaves.* — Ernie J. Zelinski

And here's something equally ridiculous: Even in our clean, modern, safe, well-lighted, OSHA-inspected, ergonomic cubicle-warrens we still live our lives by the time clock and the arbitrary schedules originally developed to serve the factory — long after time clocks and rigid schedules have in many cases outlived their usefulness!

Certainly some businesses *do* have legitimate needs for rigid schedules. If you're a waiter in a busy restaurant, you want to know your relief will be there for you *on time*. If you're running an assembly line, you really can't just have your human "components" wandering in and out of the factory at will. If you're running a Wal-Mart, it's got to open, with sufficient employees in place, at the scheduled hour. A "civilized" world will probably never be without clocks and schedules. But how many of us unquestioningly live by the clock and the schedule — when there's no well-grounded need to?

Wouldn't many of us be better off chucking the clock and tending to our work, our avocations, and our families on a more flexible schedule? Absolutely! But the holy clock, the tightly defined shift, the routine, the demand of the machine has become society's habit. It's "the way things are done." "Can't fight city hall." "Don't rock the boat." "Take the path of least resistance."

Other aspects of the rigidly scheduled post-Industrial Job Culture make even less sense. They're not only pointless, but pointlessly destructive. For instance why — with the horrendous traffic congestion in places like Silicon Valley, Seattle's eastside, Los Angeles, and the various commuter routes into Boston and New York City — should so many businesses continue to force fixed, traditional, 9-to-5 or 8-to-5 schedules on employees?

Point to ponder

Throughout most of human history, leisure was prized for its own sake — because only with ample leisure did individuals have time for philosophy, socialization, creativity, and community participation.

Today, we've "improved" to the point where leisure — within strict limits! — is grudgingly accepted because it makes us more contented and efficient in the workplace. Are we better off because of this attitude?

Given options such as flexible scheduling or telecommuting, most companies make only token gestures in the direction of surrendering rigidity. Even with highways jammed, the air brown with vehicle emissions, and their employees frantic and harried, few companies are willing to chuck the whole notion of rigid schedules. Even with workers just a phone call, an e-mail, or a teleconference away, most companies still demand those who receive company paychecks to work on site — even when there is no practical reason for it whatsoever — even when all they're doing is preserving a structure designed to make factories more efficient a century or more ago!

> *If hard work were such a wonderful thing, surely the rich would have kept it all to themselves.* — Lane Kirkland

It's strange how, once something becomes customary, we cling to it — and even passionately defend it — long after it's outlived any legitimate purpose. Just as most Americans probably imagine the two-party political system, time zones, or income taxes are eternal absolutes, woven into the very fabric of reality, most probably never even consider that the fundamental rules and rhythms by which they live are actually unnatural and unhealthy — not to mention 100-years obsolete!

But although the majority of the well-schooled populace fails to question the tyranny of the Job Culture, even as millions hate and suffer from their jobs, many people — both workers and intellectuals — *have* questioned and criticized from the beginning.

Chapter Two The Classic Case Against Jobs

It usually begins with Ned Lud. Who might never have existed.

Frustrated factory worker Lud might (or might not) have smashed a couple of frames used to automate the manufacture of stockings shortly after the dawn of the Industrial Revolution. Whatever he did (or didn't) do in real life, by 1811 Ned Lud had morphed into the legendary "King Ludd" or "Captain Ludd." And thus he hammered his way into history.

The mythic captain founded and led a very real workers' revolt. His followers attacked the equipment and factories of the early industrial age. They broke into mills. They smashed looms. They revolted against destruction of the handcrafting economy they had known. They revolted against the dawning Industrial Revolution itself.

Angry workers created such havoc in Britain during the era of the Napoleonic Wars that at one point His Majesty's government had more troops deployed against England's own workers than against the French empire-builders.

Two hundred years later, if machinery or technology makes you uneasy, someone is sure to label you a Luddite.

Historians differ about what the Luddites were actually so upset about. Was it the obsolescence of skilled trades? Was it imposition of an economic system they considered unfair? Was it loss of individual autonomy? The destruction of their familiar way of life? All of the above — and more?

One thing is certain: The machinery that made goods more affordable and eventually raised the level of prosperity throughout the industrialized world lured (or compelled) farmers and herders away from the land. The Industrial Revolution took lives that had been lived "organically," according to the seasons, the weather, the tasks at hand, and family and community rhythms, and savagely regimented them.

All the pains, privations (and benefits) outlined in Chapter One became the reality for people who had only recently lived more like this:

> The work pattern was one of alternate bouts of intense labour and of idleness. A weaver, for example, might weave eight or nine yards on a rainy day. On other days, a contemporary diary tells us, he might weave just two yards before he did "sundry jobs about the lathe and in the yard; wrote a letter in the evening." Or he might go cherry-picking, work on a community dam, calve the cow, cut down trees or go to watch a public hanging.[1]

Once again it's important to note that such a life was hardly paradise (certainly not for the poor brigands who provided the entertainment at public hangings). It's easy for scribblers like me to exult about living by the natural rhythm of the seasons or the joy of laboring on the land. But just throw one of us rhapsodizers out into a blizzard or make us kneel in the mud

---

[1] Hodgkinson, Tom. "The Virtue of Idleness." *The Guardian*. August 7, 2004. Hodgkinson is quoting historian E.P. Thompson from his book *The Making of the English Working Class.*

of a springtime garden and dig worms, and reality looks a little less idyllic. Ask us to *earn a living* under such conditions and we'll be the first to run for civilization. The "joys" of handcrafting were likewise often backbreaking and not very profitable.

Nevertheless, the Industrial Revolution brought about wrenching disruption. It destroyed a longstanding way of life. Above all, *it took control of individual work lives away from ordinary individuals and placed that power into the hands of wealthy individuals and impersonal institutions.* It did this even as it gradually raised prosperity and improved standards of living.

From those days of disruption into these days of anomie and antidepressants, most people have hated jobs. The workers themselves have hated jobs. Philosophers have hated jobs. Reformers have hated jobs — and tried to make them more palatable.

Over the last two centuries, there have been many arguments made against industrialization and the Job Culture. Anti-job positions range from the pragmatic to the wildly idealistic, from the civil to the uncivilized.

> *What work I have done I have done because it has been play. If it had been work I shouldn't have done it. Who was it who said, "Blessed is the man who has found his work"? Whoever it was he had the right idea in his mind. Mark you, he says his work — not somebody else's work. The work that is really a man's own work is play and not work at all. Cursed is the man who has found some other man's work and cannot lose it. When we talk about the great workers of the world we really mean the great players of the world. The fellows who groan and sweat under the weary load of toil that they bear never can hope to do anything great. How can*

they when their souls are in a ferment of revolt against the employment of their hands and brains? The product of slavery, intellectual or physical, can never be great.
— Mark Twain

Arguments range from Bertrand Russell's learned philosophical writings *In Praise of Idleness* to the wish expressed by members of the neo-paleolithic or neo-primitivist movements that humans give up *all* technology, retreat to the Stone Age, and try the whole experiment of civilization all over again from scratch — if they try it at all.[2]

Here are a few of the typical arguments against job-holding and the Job Culture, as expressed by a variety of philosophers from Karl Marx to contemporary neo-primitivist John Zerzan. I'm merely listing these positions, not endorsing most of them.

- Job-holding enriches powerful, wealthy capitalists at the expense of exploited workers.
- Industrial and post-industrial corporate methods are leading to a catastrophic imbalance between rich and poor, first world and third world.
- Large corporate enterprises are inherently more powerful than individuals or small enterprises, and more able to control government through money and other means of influence.
- Getting "back to the land" is more healthy for society than industrial work.
- Industrial and post-industrial society encourages mindless consumerism, rather than solid, community-based values.

---

[2] These extreme technophobes are strangely eager to use computers, printing presses, radio, and television to further their quest to destroy all computers, printing presses, radio, and television. What's amazing is that so many owners of the aforesaid media are eager to give their avowed enemies wide publicity.

- The industrial and post-industrial economy is destroying the environment.
- Redistribution of wealth is needed if we are to live up to our ideals of equality. Society must be more "leveled," without vast distinctions between workers and capitalists.
- Sedentary, repetitive work is deadening to both body and soul.
- If outsiders control the economic fate of your community, then those outsiders have more say over your lifestyle, your future, and your economic well-being than you do.
- Technology, automation, and industrialization are destroying more jobs than they create.
- Power in the world is increasingly passing into the hands of a wealthy globalist oligarchy, whose members care for nothing except lining their own pockets by any means necessary.

I personally think a few of these arguments have merit and some are total hogwash. Try to "level" everyone and you'll merely end up with an entire culture that suffers because the smart, able people have either been crushed or forced to rise through ruthlessness or sneaky subterfuge. We already saw that bitter experiment at work in Russia, China, and most cruelly of all, Pol Pot's Cambodia of the 1970s.

On the other hand, some of these arguments make good points. One of the great modern libertarians, Karl Hess (1923-1994), allied himself with the new-left to preach (and live) a sensible, community-centered technology. He used the argument that if outside forces control your economic destiny, then they control you. Instead of sitting in an ivory tower issuing airy theories (ala Marx and Zerzan), he pitched in and created new, local, more humane work systems. And on his limited, experimental basis, his ideas worked. Hess' books, *Commu-*

nity Technology and *Dear America* are a bit dated and highly idealistic, but still well worth reading by anyone who seeks a different life and a saner, more balanced world.

> *I like work: it fascinates me. I can sit and look at it for hours.* — Jerome K Jerome

Many traditional arguments against job-holding reflect a Dickensian age of dark, smoky factories, child labor, and 12-hour (or even 16-hour) days. Those arguments made more sense in the era when millions labored under the tyranny of cruel overseers hired by distant "robber barons."

Nevertheless, with global conglomerates replacing true independent businesses today, the "little guy" is very much in danger of being exploited — not necessarily in the Marxian sense, but in the sense of being deprived of autonomy primarily for some outsider's purposes — purposes that bring the individual little direct reward, other than monetary.

One example: Wal-Mart may be a consumer wonderland, but when it's become the only place in town that you can get a job — and when you're just one more utterly replaceable "human resource" among thousands — the corporation's advantage over you is incalculable.

Another: Larry Ellison, CEO of the database giant Oracle, has made himself fabulously wealthy and has made his company astonishingly powerful — largely by enabling government agencies, corporate data-miners, and the like to track and analyze the activities of millions of innocent people — people who have absolutely no say in what's being done to them. Has Ellison improved the world with his products? Or is he — in those no-longer-fashionable nineteenth-century phrases — a "robber baron" and an "exploiter of the downtrodden masses"? You be the judge.

The same question could be asked of many other individuals and companies. Does Halliburton — that great beneficiary of oil wars — bless or exploit society? Yes, that ultimate politically connected corporation (with its dizzying array of subsidiaries) "provides jobs" and probably even treats its employees well. But is the world better or worse because of that giant company's methods?

And how about CitiBank? McDonalds? General Motors? For every plus one can name, someone else can point to an example of such companies doing harm — whether to employees, customers, communities, families, the environment, or in some cases, even entire countries.

Valid or invalid, the most surprising thing is that virtually all the classic arguments against jobs and the Job Culture come from the so-called left. They come from socialists, communists, left-anarchists, or the sorts of do-gooders who infest Nanny States everywhere, imposing top-down "reforms" that only create more problems than they solve.

Libertarians and conservatives (who ought to be shouting against knee-jerk job-holding and the Job Culture as vigorously as anyone) are often either silent on this subject or so busy writing paeans to free market that they forget to notice that the system they're promoting is no longer truly free, freedom-enhancing, or truly market-driven.

The real case against the Job Culture and the mass practice of highly structured job holding in the twenty-first century ought to be made by and for free-market individualists.

Chapter Three The Free-Market Case Against Jobs

Conservatives and many libertarians tend to support the business world quite uncritically. If you're not "pro-business" (many of these supporters of free enterprise say), then you must be "pro-government," "pro-regulation," and "anti-freedom."

But this attitude is another example of the kind of disconnect the Job Culture has conditioned us to. The Job Culture and mass job-holding don't support freedom. They're *destroying* freedom.

Indeed, entrepreneurial ventures, truly free markets, and various forms of independent income-earning *can* and do support freedom. But that's not what we have in the institution-dominated business world of today.

Institutional systems, whether government or nominally private, demand a similar mindset and behavior from those who live under them: obedience to authority, surrender to arbitrary rules and regulations, acceptance of the idea that the individual is just one small (and usually interchangeable) cog in a larger system. Both government and private institutions use top-down, command-and-control structures, and actively diminish individual responsibility and innovation (even as they hope to benefit from outstanding individual talents).

And increasingly, today, these two supposedly different (and supposedly adversarial) forms of institution, government and private, are merging into one freedom-stealing force.

But we're still free, so far.

Oh yes, we members of the Job Culture have the freedom to consume to our hearts' content and to go as deeply into debt as lenders, encouraged by Federal Reserve policies and federal commerce controls will allow us to go. Yes, we have the freedom to buy cheap goods increasingly made in cheap-labor countries (thanks in part to such very unfree "free-trade" organizations as NAFTA and the WTO).

Yes, we have the freedom to travel on the highways we pay for — as long as we obtain the proper government documentation and purchase all the government-required, privately provided products, from insurance policies to onboard black boxes (which those friendly corporate automakers installed without telling us). We're free to travel on the roads as long as we can afford the price tag of privately produced vehicles whose prices are eternally driven upward by government regulations — regulations that are often approved and sometimes even written by private industry associations.

And, of course, we have the freedom to travel on privately run "public transportation," as long as we submit to warrantless searches by either federal or private screeners. And those helpful "private" airlines will also turn over every scrap of data on us so the government can decide who should be "allowed" to fly.

We have the freedom to own our own home, as long as that home meets institutionalized standards set by various professional guilds, and rubber-stamped by various government agencies. And as long as we pay both our mortgage and our taxes.

Yes, we have the freedom to work — as long as we pee in a bottle, march to our employer's drummer, don't express unpopular opinions, show our government ID number, and surrender more than 1/3 of our work lives to the ever-grasping taxman.

If we screw up, we even have the opportunity to spend the next decade or so of our lives hosted by a private prison-operating corporation, after being delivered into their hands by a tax-paid justice system. And those private prison operators even have their own lobbying groups to ensure that they get more and more opportunity to serve us. (In small, dying towns throughout America, too, prisons have become one of the few growth industries, replacing productive activities. Counties and cities that once clamored to be the next railroad terminus or host the next electronics plant now beg to be let in on the act of helping the U.S. imprison a larger portion of its population than any other nation in the world. Why? Because it's *good for business!*)

We are the most free people on earth. Everybody knows it. And we owe it all to the combination of "good government" and institutional, Job Culture-driven "free enterprise."

You bet genuine free-marketeers should be among the first and loudest to protest this form of business-as-usual!

A mindset of submission

Submission to the endless rules of institutions is the same, whether those institutions are run from boardrooms or bureaucratic agencies. Obedience to authority is obedience to authority, no matter which authority we choose to bow before. Surrendering self-ownership is surrendering self-ownership, whether you give yourself up to Global MegaCorp, Inc. or surrender your authority over your life to Rule No. 762.32(A)(1)(b) of Federal Agency XYZ.

Once you're in the habit of giving up independence, you'll give it up to anybody who threatens you with a big enough stick or dangles a tasty enough carrot in front of your nose.

And while there is a vast difference between dealing with a small entrepreneur and a vast government bureaucracy, there's precious little (and *increasingly* little) difference between dealing with a vast corporate bureaucracy and a vast government bureaucracy.

Enormous, complex, bureaucratic, top-down government is different from enormous, complex, bureaucratic, top-down corporate industry only in the source of its funding and in government's ability to use overt force to get its way. And while I admit that the ability to tax and the ability to kill and jail people definitely marks a huge difference between governmental and private institutions, it's less of a difference than we might think (even without private corporations running government prisons).

Other examples of the private/government business connection — a connection which has gone far beyond what Dwight Eisenhower warned was a dangerous "military-industrial complex":

- When industry devotes itself to producing tools (like tanks and bombs) used only by government, or when it accepts millions of dollars in tax-paid funding, business might as well be a branch of government.
- When governments use the International Monetary Fund, the World Trade Organization, or the World Bank to force countries to accept the presence and practices of multi-national corporations, governments are behaving like particularly brutal marketing departments for business.

And sometimes you simply cannot tell where private enterprise begins and government ends. What, for instance, is Amtrak? Or Fannie Mae? Or Freddie Mac? What is the Corporation for Public Service that runs the AmeriCorps program? What is the Corporation for Public Broadcasting? What is the Federal Reserve Board? All are some mind-boggling government-private hybrid.

For instance, the Federal Reserve Board has a government-appointed chairman and sets monetary policy for the entire country. But "the Fed" takes advantage of its status as a "private" organization to avoid any serious audit of its operations. Amtrak operates privately — but only because taxpayer dollars keep its ever-failing operations alive decade after decade. Fannie Mae and Freddie Mac, that cute pair who are, as I write these words, leading us toward the debacle of a housing bubble, are both listed on the New York Stock Exchange — but were created for social-engineering purposes by the federal government and remain intimately entangled with government in their every operation.[1]

The relationship between the institution of large, central government and large, centralized business is so close that to call it incestuous would be an understatement. Hydra-headed would be more like it.

Evil twins

It's no coincidence, and should be no surprise, that private institutional structures and governmental institutional structures are so similar and tend to work so closely together. It is not an aberration or a perversion of the business world, as many free marketeers like to think. It is also not new.

---

1 For more on Fannie Mae and Freddie Mac see: White, Lawrence J. "Cato Policy Analysis No. 528: Fannie Mae, Freddie Mac, and Housing Finance: Why True Privatization is Good Public Policy." October 7, 2004. http://www.cato.org/pubs/pas/pa-528es.html

Big, all-controlling government and the large institutions of the Industrial Revolution were born together, from the same roots, for many of the same purposes — to regiment, centralize, homogenize, and control. To succeed in their purposes, both needed to turn a population of rowdy, diverse individuals into a compliant, largely robotic, mass. And — it's horrible, but undeniable — big government and many big corporate institutions were created side-by-side as two facets of one increasingly formidable war-making machine.

It didn't "just happen" that two allegedly diverse institutions came together for the same purpose at the same time. And it doesn't "just happen" today that those same institutions continue to reinforce each other in war and peace.

There is another institution – also born at the same time and for the same reasons — that reinforces the corporate-government institutional mindset. I'm talking about government schooling.

Compulsory institutionalized schooling is the nymph or larval stage of the Job Culture cockroach. And the larval stage of tyranny.

> *Work — other people's work — is an intolerable idea to a cat. Can you picture cats herding sheep or agreeing to pull a cart? They will not inconvenience themselves to the slightest degree.* — Dr. Louis J. Camuti

Schooled to conformity

In 1806, Prussian forces were resoundingly defeated by Napoleon at the Battle of Jena. Prussia, which considered itself a mighty and modern state, reeled. But Prussia was not merely a state. It was one of the first *police states* — a new type of government well suited to the emerging industrial age.

"Police state" was not then a synonym for tyranny, as we use it today. It was a modern and "enlightened" new form of government in which "experts," using "scientific principles," were entitled to run every aspect of citizens' lives via a rigid, top-down, hierarchy.

When Prussia suffered humiliating defeat, its policy-setters and bureaucrats had the power to ensure that no such catastrophe occurred again. They built a system of compulsory schooling to enable all of their society to be rapidly mobilized to conduct efficient, effective warfare. This system aimed to produce three types of citizens:

- Willing, well-ordered factory workers.
- Orderly subordinates for bureaucratic service.
- Obedient soldiers.

In a little over a decade, Prussia had its new school system functioning. That system featured:

- Compulsory attendance.
- Classes segregated by age.
- Subjects rigidly segmented.
- Rigidly defined hours of study, controlled by bells.
- Authoritarian teachers standing before rows of silent, obedient students.
- Rote memorization.
- Artificial measures of achievement (e.g. grades).

If that structure sounds familiar, it's again no accident. As early as 1819, American education reformers had made trips to Prussia and returned to sing the praises of the new system.

The Prussian ideas and ideals spread rapidly among American educators, legislators, and social-welfare reformers. Some U.S. advocates of the Prussian system openly advocated the same worker-bureaucrat-soldier outcome as the Prussian educrats did. Others spoke of the need to rapidly homogenize the nation's increasingly diverse immigrant population. They spoke of reducing (or even entirely eliminating!) crime by getting the "foreign element" under control. Others were entranced by the "scientific management" of human beings — never mind that the "science" they used was the absurd and now thoroughly discredited pseudo-science of phrenology.[2]

Within a few decades, the United States went from having mostly private, customized education to having compulsory attendance and ever-longer school hours and school years in government institutions. In some cases, children even had to be driven to government institutions at gunpoint — driven away from angry, protesting parents who resented the virtual imprisonment of their children.

You'll find the story of America's police-state school system in John Taylor Gatto's *Underground History of American Education* and in Sheldon Richman's *Separating School and State*. You'll also find an abbreviated version of it in *The State vs. the People: The Rise of the American Police State*, which I co-wrote with Aaron Zelman.[3]

For all the periodic "reforms" of the U.S. school system, and for all its cosmetic changes (and its dumbing down) over time, the system we enter today as malleable little five-year-olds is built on the Prussian police-state principle. Critics complain that today's schools fail to educate children. But that's no surprise; education was never the goal.

The goal was to prepare us for our role in the Job Culture. And the Job Culture is a means to utilize individuals to further

---

2 Phrenologists claimed to be able to read a person's mental capabilities and moral character simply by studying the shape of the individual's skull and the various bumps and dents upon it.

3 Mazel Freedom Press, PO Box 270014, Hartford, WI 53027, www.jpfo.org/tsvtp.htm

the aims of state and mega-corporations without rebellion or messy individuality.

So the Job Culture begins for us long before we actually get our first job. And we're stuck in it until the day we die.

Independence fosters freedom

James Madison, the father of the Bill of Rights, wrote in 1792:

> The class of citizens, who provide at once their own food and their own raiment, may be viewed as the most truly independent and happy. They are more: They are the best basis of public liberty, and the strongest bulwark of public safety. It follows, that the greater the proportion of this class to the whole society, the more free, the more independent, and the more happy must be the society itself.[4]

Madison was speaking specifically about independent farmers, but both he and his friend Thomas Jefferson (who helped spur creation of the Bill of Rights) were believers in the independent farmer *and* the independent entrepreneur — and for the same reasons.

They knew that people who can provide for themselves are far less likely to march in lockstep, far more likely to think for themselves, and far more capable of independent action than those whose first aim is to appease institutional gods.

> *It is a well-known fact that although the public is fine when taken individually, when it forms itself into large groups, it tends to act as though it has one partially consumed Pez tablet for a brain.* — Dave Barry

---

4 Madison, James. *National Gazette*. March 3, 1792. Quoted in Hartmann, Thom. *Unequal Protection: The Rise of Corporate Dominance and the Theft of Human Rights*. Rodale, 2002.

The assumption that we have both the ability and responsibility to take care of ourselves and (when need be) our fellows, is quite simply a keystone of freedom. Without individual responsibility and initiative, we cannot remain free.

And we need that sense of responsibility and initiative to extend to every aspect of our lives if we are to retain (or restore) freedom. We must not just take initiative on a project or a volunteer effort; initiative should be a basic assumption of our lives. We should not just assume responsibility over a decision or a job; responsibility for our own choices must be the bedrock on which our existence is built.

> *The highest manifestation of life consists in this: that a being governs its own actions. A thing which is always subject to the direction of another is somewhat of a dead thing.* — Saint Thomas Aquinas

In the world of business, entrepreneurship or self-employment is the ultimate form of taking responsibility. The more we take the responsibility to provide for our own welfare, the more independent we become from those who prefer to control us.

Living in the Job Culture has conditioned us to taking a "someone else will deal with it" mentality. And if "someone else" is responsible, then we, by definition, are not.

A "right" to be free of big business?

Libertarians who count the great thinker Jefferson among their heroes may be surprised to learn that he wanted the Bill of Rights to include a proscription against monopoly businesses.

The Industrial Revolution was only getting underway in Jefferson's day; he didn't have our modern experience with thousands of large-scale industrial (or post-industrial), politically connected business institutions. But he and the rest of the American colonists had extensive, and bitter, experience with one of the first big government-favored corporate endeavors, the East India Company.

The East India Company had been granted enormous powers over trade between Britain and the U.S. It was a small matter of that company's unfair control of tea imports that helped turn colonists into enterprising smugglers, and eventually led to that famous act of monkeywrenching, dumping tons of tea into Boston harbor. (The Boston Tea Party was not precisely over a tax, as we were taught in school, but over the government in London favoring one large business to the point of strangling many small, domestic, entrepreneurial businesses and forcing productive citizen-merchants to become outlaw smugglers.)

As a result of his study, his experiences, and his own nature, Jefferson developed an extreme distrust for three institutions: big government, organized religion, and what he called the "pseudo aristoi" — that is, wealthy, powerful individuals, and the privileged business establishment.[5]

Today conservatives remember only the first of Jefferson's deep distrusts. Libertarians tend to remember the first and second. Only "left-wingers" remember how profoundly Jefferson disliked and distrusted all but the smallest, most entrepreneurial business enterprises.

Should an anti-monopoly provision have been included in the Bill of Rights? Most conservatives and libertarians would howl "NO!" They'd see an anti-monopoly amendment as in infringement on free markets and the right of association. Nevertheless, Jefferson's fear and distrust of the "psuedo aristoi" and monopolies applies equally well today when one

---

[5] More on Jefferson's view of business can be found in *Unequal Protection*, by Thom Hartmann.

looks at the large international companies that increasingly receive benefits from government and give their allegiance in return *to* government.

> **Point to ponder**
> Today, large corporations are not only imposing the Job Culture upon workers of the industrial and post-industrial west. They're also virtually dictating policy and cultural change to the nations of the world through institutions like the International Monetary Fund and the World Bank, trumping existing local cultures and business models with the models of the Industrial Revolution and post-industrial western society.
> The world is poorer for this kind of conformity, even when some workers are economically enriched. And tragically, "enrichment" via huge international loans and the obligations imposed along with those loans, has actually disrupted, and in some cases bankrupted, the economies of many small nations while enriching the highly favored global corporations that swoop in to manage development.[6]

Yes, we receive benefits from all this. Specific businesses can be productive or destructive, ethical or unethical, freedom-enhancing or freedom-destroying. Much of what business accomplishes is positive.

We are not cruelly exploited Dickensian orphans. Although we waste an extraordinary portion of our lives being

---

[6] The BBC offers a basic (and largely favorable) description of the IMF and world bank here: news.bbc.co.uk/1/hi/business/the_economy/economy_reports/95218.stm. The organization The Global Policy Forum monitors all international policy-making efforts. They print both favorable and unfavorable articles about the IMF here: www.globalpolicy.org/socecon/bwi-wto/imfind.htm. Articles about the World Bank: www.globalpolicy.org/socecon/bwi-wto/bankind.htm. Articles about the World Trade Organization: www.globalpolicy.org/socecon/bwi-wto/indexwto.htm.

schooled[7], we receive a better payoff than our great-grandfathers did.

Nevertheless, we have lost so much of our personal independence that most of us never even try to comprehend what our great-great-great grandparents surrendered. We have become so used to our bondage that we don't even perceive it as such.

> *The opposite of bravery is not cowardice but conformity.* — Robert Anthony

The person conditioned to being a cog in the wheel of institutional schooling — scrambling at the sound of bells, sitting in regimented rows, dropping his interests at 50-minute intervals to obey the bleatings of Authority about the next subject on Authority's schedule — makes a very easy leap to thinking of himself as a cog in the corporate-business wheel.

The person who spends the majority of her years as a cog in a schooling wheel and a cog in a work wheel doesn't have to go far at all to become a cog-in-the-wheel "good citizen," loyal to and dependent upon the largess and authority of the state, rather than on the principles of liberty.

Now, in the best of all worlds, a "good citizen" is one who asks questions, who demands answers, who refuses to put up with institutionalized arrogance or patronizing "leaders" (leaders who are really only supposed to be representatives). A truly good citizen — that is, one whose actions enhance liberty and individuality — understands in her deepest heart one of Jefferson's other beliefs: that citizens should rise up and kick ass early and often.

---

[7] It's estimated that a typical individual can learn all the basics of reading, writing, and math in about 100 hours. A person who has those skills can self-teach everything else, or seek teachers and fellow learners.

"I hold it, that a little rebellion, now and then, is a good thing, and necessary in the political world as storms in the physical."

Even though libertarians, conservatives, and "left-wingers" may disagree vehemently on their reasons for opposing the Job Culture, all ought to be united in getting rid of this blight that afflicts individuals, families, communities and nations.

But now ...enough background. If you're angered by all this unfreedom, if you're fed up with what you experience every day, it's time to start changing things.

But where do we begin? We begin with the thing we can most readily change: ourselves.

Part II
Freeing Ourselves

Gone to Croatoan

"Gone to Croatoan"
That is what I'll answer
When somebody asks me
"Where have you been?" Just gone
Dancing with the wild folk
Roanoke-ing into
The deserts of August
Mystifying those who
Go on thinking they must
Work, work, work at something.

They bow down to Cronos.
Their hours becoming tithes;
Their factories, temples.
They move to a 5/2
Industrial rhythm
From Monday to Friday.
Saturday and Sunday
They suck on a houka
Inhaling their leisure.
Just another seizure
Of their precious time.

"Stopping by the woods"
That is what I'll say
When they ask, "What's yer line?"
My work and play, both fun
My days have become one.

Nothing I call weekend,
Nor any nine to five
I say carpe diem
And play, play, play to live.
— Keith Perkins[1]

---

1 © 2005 by Keith Perkins. Used by permission. "Gone to Croatoan" or "Gone to Croatan" was a cryptic message found at the site of the lost Roanoke Colony. History books tell us that the first English colonists, left on the Virginia coast by Sir Walter Raleigh in 1587, probably died of disease or starvation or were massacred. The message – and various local folklore – tells us that the "lost" colonists may have in fact become the first European-American dropouts, abandoning European-style civilization to live with the Indians.

Chapter Four
Getting a Goal

As I write these words, I'm sitting at a hand-made pine computer desk in a one-room cabin on a hilltop. There's not a single neighbor within sound or sight. I glance out my window and I see, on one side, tall evergreen trees against a gray sky. Where the trees part, my eye travels down to a valley 400 feet below. Mists curl above green pastures. Beyond the valley rise blue hills.

This is where I live and work. It's been 10 years since I attended a business meeting. Ten years since I had to don a pair of pantyhose. Ten years since I ate a day-old sandwich out of a vending machine. I can't remember the last time I sat in a traffic jam or cooled my heels outside the office of an executive who kept everyone waiting mainly to reassure himself of his power over others.

Ten years ago, I led a pretty good life, actually. I had a nice little house in a pleasant, slow-paced city. I had a dog. I had flexible freelancer's hours and a nearby inland beach to walk on. But I also had debts and phone tag and my clients' corporate cultures to deal with.

Ten years before that I worked as much as 20 hours a day and had nothing except the money I earned (and spent) hand over fist. Oh yes, I also owned a "status" townhouse and had bragging rights to the most "exciting" (e.g. demanding, unpredictable, exhausting, often quite chaotic) job anyone in my working-class family had ever had. It was pretty impressive for a kid who'd barely made it out of high school. And I was miserable. The main thing that lifestyle taught me, once I got over the sheer ego boost of having stumbled into such a position, was how much I wanted something entirely different.

It's been a long way from here to there. And not necessarily on a straight course. I had to do a lot of things I *didn't* want to do to get to where I ultimately wanted to get. But today, as I look out that window onto the green-blue landscape below, I'm very close to where I always dreamed of being.

The life I have may be entirely different than the life you want. But no matter what you want to achieve, you have options — both in choosing your goal and in choosing your techniques for getting there.

Everybody has a chance — with a lot of creativity, some initiative, and a little bit of luck — to approach a better life. A life outside the job trap. A life where work and all the things that work is *supposed* to support are in more harmonious balance. That's true even if you're currently in a very difficult spot.

> *Unemployment is capitalism's way of getting you to plant a garden.* — Orson Scott Card

Each of us also has *barriers* to reaching our dreams. We have obstacles to overcome — and we'll examine a few of those later. But for now let's stop and look beyond those barriers and gaze toward the life we'd like to achieve.

Can't get anywhere without a goal

You probably won't achieve your goal of a better life unless you have a dream of a better life.

It's possible, of course, that aliens will come along and kidnap you out of your dreary life into a better one. Or that a billionaire uncle will conveniently die and leave everything to you. Or that you'll be walking along a beach someday and find an odd-shaped bottle that ...

But really, even under those fantastic circumstances, if you don't know what you truly want, deep down, chances are you'll just squander your opportunities.

Having a vision — a goal — an objective — is the first step to getting from here to ...somewhere. Goals, however, can function in ways as mysterious as the denizens of peculiarly shaped bottles.

> *Too many people are thinking of security instead of opportunity. They seem more afraid of life than death.*
> — James F. Byrnes

In the classic how-to book, you're told to set a goal, then move step-by-logical-patient-step toward it. That works for some people. It might work for you if you tend to be a linear thinker and a methodical actor.

But a goal can also be an almost mystical-magical thing. Sometimes merely holding a vision of what you want to achieve is life-changing in itself — even when you can't immediately march step-to-step to get there.

The biographies of writers, artists, and mathematicians are full of instances in which the person set out to achieve something, worked very hard at it, got nowhere ... then solved the problem while stepping onto a bus, biting into a cocktail weenie, or dreaming about flying to the moon. At that "aha!" moment, the thinker or artist receives an insight that's crucial to further success. The insight wasn't achieved through any linear process, but nevertheless, it was the result of all the work, thinking, and planning that came before it.

> *A man is not idle because he is absorbed in thought. There is a visible labor and there is an invisible labor.*
> — Victor Hugo

However you get there, whether on a straight course or a twisty, unpredictable one, the first step to freeing yourself from the job trap and minimizing the effects of the Job Culture is:

Know what you want to achieve.

Three factors in springing the job trap

Your harmonious, balanced future life will have three basic aspects:

- Your work
- Your workstyle
- Your lifestyle.

These three may blend seamlessly into each other. Or you may have distinct separations (for instance, between workstyle and lifestyle). But in an ideal life, all three elements are in healthy balance.

Let's start by defining these terms. Then let's go on to a simple exercise in goal setting that takes all three of these life elements into consideration.

Defining the terms

Your Work is the activity you perform either 1) to earn enough money to live on or 2) to form a solid center or sense of purpose in your life.

Sometimes work fulfills only one of those roles, sometimes both.

> *A good rule of thumb is if you've made it to thirty-five and your job still requires you to wear a name tag, you've made a serious vocational error.* — Dennis Miller

If you're one of the fortunate few who doesn't have to earn a living, then doing work you care about is still important because having a vocation raises us out of boredom, ennui, and a sense of uselessness.

On the other hand, if your skills or circumstances limit you to doing a job you don't love and you have no driving passion that will lead you to more satisfying work, that's a shame. In that case, your goal would be to try to minimize the dominance of that job in your life.[1]

For most of us — who *must* work but who crave satisfaction — the goal is for work to be both financially and psychologically rewarding.

Your workstyle is *the way you perform your work.* This can cover a lot of territory. Workstyle covers **external factors**, such as whether you have a long commute, work in an office, or have to attend a lot of meetings. It also covers **subjective preferences**, such as whether you prefer excitement and

---

[1] However, please don't be too quick to conclude that you can't get out of a bad job. Even if you don't see the way out *now*, or even if you don't have faith in your own abilities, having a solid desire to find something better can be a powerful force for change.

stimulation in your job or whether you'd rather have meditative peace.

Your workstyle will also take into consideration your own **personal habits**.

For instance, if you're lazy and easily distracted — as I unfortunately am — your workstyle goals will have to take your procrastinating habits into consideration. When listing your workstyle goals in our upcoming exercise, you might make a notation that you'll need to create a daily schedule for yourself or to disconnect your computer from the Internet (and all its distractions) during work hours.

On the other hand, if you're such a high-intensity, high-focus person that you feel you're neglecting your health or your family, you *also* might make a notation on your goal sheet to create a daily schedule for yourself — but unlike lazy, procrastinating me, your schedule will be designed to push you away from work and toward exercise, family time, or yardwork, instead of being designed to make you crack down on yourself.

Your lifestyle, the third life aspect we'll include in our exercise, encompasses two factors: **everything you do outside of work** and **the totality of the way you live, *including* your work.**

If those two points sound contradictory — lifestyle is everything but work and lifestyle is everything *including* work — they're really not. Think of it this way: work is (usually) a separate activity from family time, leisure, community activism, etc. But work is also part of that larger thing called life.

> *Don't sacrifice your life to work and ideals. The most important things in life are human relations. I found that out too late.* — Katharinde Susannah Prichard

For purposes of the exercise we're about to undertake, we'll focus on the first definition: lifestyle covers non-work activities. Just keep in mind that work, workstyle, and lifestyle all fit within the one great institution called Your Life, and that the ideal is for them all to perform together in harmony — for YOU.

> *Work for something because it is good, not just because it stands a chance to succeed.* — Vaclav Havel

An exercise in whole-life goal-setting

Take a standard-sized sheet of notebook paper. Draw a square in the middle of it about three inches across. Starting at the top of the square, draw a straight line that runs up to the top of the page. Starting at the lower right corner of the page, draw a straight line that runs to the edge of the square. Then draw another line that runs from the lower left corner of the page to the edge of the square.

Your drawing will look something like the one on page 66, only bigger:

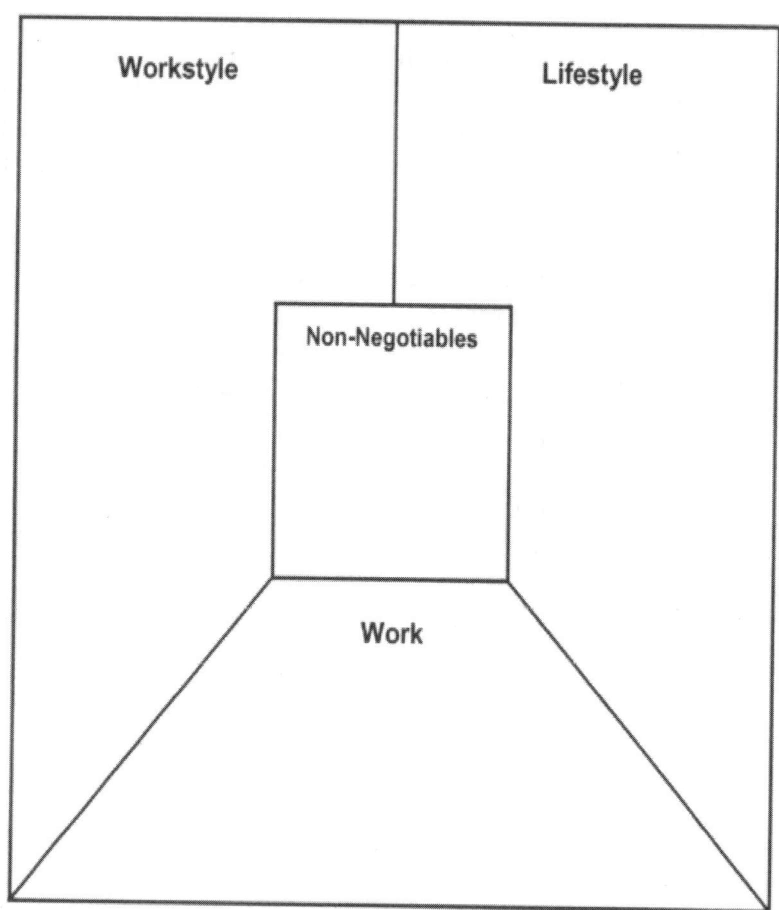

You've just created four segments. In small print, somewhere unobtrusive, label those segments.

- Label the inner square "Non-Negotiables"
- Label the lowest wedge "Work"
- Label the left-hand wedge "Workstyle"
- Label the right-hand wedge "Lifestyle"

Now you're going to start brainstorming about how you want your future life to look.

Leave the center box blank for the moment and begin filling the other three with brief statements about the things you want in each of those areas.

Don't worry about doing things in any particular order. Just write things down as they come to you and put them in the segment you think they should be in. There may be overlap between workstyle and lifestyle. Or between work and workstyle. Don't fret. Just let your thoughts run free.

> *Don't you wish you had a job like mine? All you have to do is think up a certain number of words! Plus, you can repeat words! And they don't even have to be true!*
> — Dave Barry

Be realistic in writing down goals: Don't write "Become a multi-millionaire" or "Be a rock star" unless you have some reasonable expectation of working your way toward that goal. Don't write "Meet Prince Charming and find everlasting ideal love" because 1) you can't control whether your prince will show up, 2) everlasting ideal love is an airy goal that will discourage you from taking nitty-gritty actions, and 3) if you live in dreamland, the real world will never satisfy you. Likewise, if you're of the opposite sexual inclination there's really no point in writing "Find a woman with a DD cup size who likes to screw all day" (that is, unless you actually do become a multi-millionaire rock star, in which case, such a woman might find you).

Focus on things you want in your work, workstyle, and life that you can take realistic steps toward.

On the other hand, don't hopelessly limit yourself, either. Even if you're currently in financial trouble, you can still aim to "Be debt free" or "Own a small farm" or "Have $10,000 in my investment portfolio in two years." Even if you're currently in a dull, dead-end job and don't have the qualifications to get out, you can still shoot for a goal like: "Own my own business," "Become a paralegal," "Do metal sculpture," or "Do work that's less taxing to my body."

Include both large and small aims ("Write a novel" and "Have a quiet corner for working" may be equally important when it comes time to reach for your goal). Just write down whatever seems desirable and "true" to you in each of the three life areas.

Include things you strongly want and things you strongly want to avoid. "I don't want my children dumbed down by government schools" is as important as "I want my children to have opportunities to experience diverse cultures." A negative desire to "Get away from this violent neighborhood" may be a bigger motivator for you than a wistful wish to "Live among self-rcliant pcople."

Take some time. Do the exercise now. If you fill up one of the segments on your piece of paper, grab another sheet and keep writing. If you have only one or two items in a segment, don't worry about it.

Keep this worksheet near you for the next week or so and add to it as new wish-list items strike you.

The items on your goal sheet must come from you. But if you're hesitant about where to begin, check the sidebar on page 72 for samples of some of the types of goals people might include on their lists.

Now, here's what to do with that still-blank center box: Anytime you think of something that is an absolute *must* for the balanced life you want to live, copy it from one of those outer segments and add it to that center box. You'll probably end up with only a handful of items in that box, but those are the ones around which everything else will revolve.

The items in the center may be work, workstyle, or lifestyle goals. All that matters is that they be at the center of what you want for your life.

If a wish-list item in one of the outer segments conflicts with one of your "musts," then you'll discard the non-essential item. If a wish-list item complements one of your "musts," you'll keep it. Later, you may also discover that some of the best wish-list items will actually help you achieve your "must" goals.

> *To fulfill a dream, to be allowed to sweat over lonely labor, to be given a chance to create, is the meat and potatoes of life. The money is the gravy.* — Bette Davis

In my case, for example, I had four "non-negotiables":

- To work as a writer or artist.
- To be freelance, neither an employee or an employer.
- To shut out a lot of society's external "noise" — ads, television, boom boxes, traffic sounds, arguments.
- To live true to my own values — never to cooperate with anything I considered to be unjust or destructive.

As you can see at a glance, there's no conflict between any of my "musts." I could pursue all four of those goals without one goal interfering with another. My central goals were mutually reinforcing, in fact. Having a quiet life makes it easier to write; being freelance makes it easier to refuse to do work I find objectionable; a writer who lives true to her values writes with more clarity because her heart isn't torn apart by conflict.

Many of my secondary objectives supported my "musts," as well. Being lazy, I wanted to work the fewest possible hours. Being a born aesthete, I wanted to live and work in a beautiful spot. Disliking crowds and traffic, I wanted to live in a rural area. Loving dogs, I wanted to be able to have a pup or three at my side while I worked.

It's possible, though, that you'll find that some of your goals conflict with others, and then you'll have to take the next step of really examining those goals and determining which take priority.

If you are in any doubt about which of your goals matter the most to you, mark each one (both in the "non-negotiables" box and in the outer wedges) with a number from 1-to-5. Fives are of utmost importance. Ones would be nice to have, but could be given up in pursuit of more important goals. Then, as you refine your goals, you'll know which matter most and which can be surrendered in the cause of winning something more vital.

> *Nothing is really work unless you would rather be doing something else.* — J.M. Barrie

But whatever you do, your venture begins with a vision of the kind of balanced life you want. Your goals needn't be carved in stone at first (or ever, for that matter). Sometimes a journey to a better life begins as nothing more than a longing, an itch for things to be different, and better, than they are.

But at some point, you have to define what "better" means to you. This exercise will help you do it. Your next-door neighbor might think that a "better" life means having more money. Your mother might think that a "better" life means you producing some grandchildren for her — *right now*. But if these aren't the goals in your own heart, they're likely to lead you into unhappiness.

Don't worry at this point about *how* to achieve your goals. All that matters for the moment is that you value these things. That you value them enough to take real steps to achieve them, rather than just dream about them.

Once you know what you want and have that vision firmly fixed in your heart and mind, you may be surprised to discover that virtually every decision you make (even decisions that don't seem specifically goal-related) will move you gradually in the direction of achieving your aim. If you're an intuitive-type decision-maker, you may move toward your goals almost unconsciously.

If you're more linear, then once you have a vision fixed firmly in your mind, you can begin planning an organized set of steps to help you get there. Again, only you can make that list, which might include anything from "get out of debt" to "get a divorce," or anything from "go back to school" to "take the kids out of school."

In Chapter Six we'll look at some general principles that will help us attain whatever variety of balanced life we're aiming for.

But first, in the next chapter, we'll look at specific work-style options that might be available to us outside the job trap. Or that might represent steps on our way out of the trap.

Help Defining Goals

If you're stuck and don't know what to list on your goal sheet, here are some examples of the sorts of things you might write, depending on your own personality and desires. As you'll see, there's some potential overlap between work and workstyle, and between workstyle and lifestyle. Don't worry about it. Put *your* goals down in the categories where *you* think they fit best.

Work goals

"To work with wood, clay, or stone."

"To pioneer the use of all-natural materials in my field."

"To sell environmentally friendly products."

"To make money making music."

"To design clothing."

"To teach."

"To work at the bleeding edge of technology."

"To have a profession that harmonizes with my values."

"To work on machinery."

"To work with my hands, instead of primarily my brain."

"To work with my brain, instead of merely my hands."

"To do work that has fewer barriers for a person with a physical disability."

"To join my husband's business."

"To be the kind of boss I always wanted to have."

Workstyle goals

"Never to sit at a desk all day."

"To work side-by-side with my partner."

"Never to drive in rush-hour traffic again."

"To make less impact on the environment."

"To work out of my home."

"To work closer to my home."

"To avoid interruptions."

"Never again to answer to a tyrannical boss."

"To make more money in less time."

"To reduce expenses by reducing costs related to job holding (e.g. extra car, gas, insurance, maintenance; work-only clothes; taxes)."

"Never to collect payroll taxes from employees."

"To have work that's mentally challenging."

"To end monotony."

Lifestyle goals

"To live near the lake."

"To work and teach my children at the same time."

"To have an adult at home with the children at all times."

"To go 'on strike' against a culture gone mad."

"To be more free to travel."

"To have time to build my own home."

"To get out of the city."

"To get involved in community theater."

"To pay less in taxes."

"To relocate to New Mexico."

"To be able to ride horses more often."

"To live on an island."

"To be able to afford a housekeeper."

"To escape the chores of my traditional gender role."

Recommended reading

The Joy of Not Working: A book for the retired, unemployed, and overworked, by Ernie J. Zelinski. Ten Speed Press, Berkeley, CA, 1997.

Chapter Five
Workstyle Options

Even if everyone reading this book held the goal of having more satisfaction in work and more balance between work and the rest of life, that goal would still mean vastly different things to people in practice.

For some, nothing will do except getting out of the conventional job world altogether. *Right now.*

Others may simply opt to work fewer or more flexible hours, or work closer to home.

Others may want a totally different profession, while the next person holding this book might want to remain in the same profession but work under more humane circumstances.

Others may want to work their way out of the job trap eventually, but feel most comfortable doing so in gradual stages.

> *The measure of a person is not in their abilities, but in their choices.* — Albus Dumbledore (aka J.K. Rowling)

For some — as Robert Frost wrote in the poem, *Two Tramps in Mud Time*, at the beginning of this book — the goal may be to have a seamless integration of work and play. Or to bring family life directly into the work place.

Others might consider that a dreadful idea. For them, work and family life should remain cleanly separated. Yet even these readers may long for work to be more *supportive* of home and family (e.g. by allowing time off for teaching children or building an addition to the family house).

Whatever its specifics, your goal will be very personal to you.

> *Personally, I have nothing against work, particularly when performed, quietly and unobtrusively, by someone else. I just don't happen to think it's an appropriate subject for an "ethic."* — Barbara Ehrenreich

The question of this chapter is: What are some of the work-style options that might enable you to establish the healthier work/life balance you crave?

Here are a few of the possibilities you can explore when considering breaking out of the trap. Keep in mind that this list isn't meant to be comprehensive, but only to give an idea of the range of options we can take advantage of.

A home-based small business

The biggest dream for most people who spring the job trap seeking greater harmony is probably to have small-scale independent work that you can do from a kitchen table, in a home workshop, or out of your own vehicle (for instance, as a handyman or gardener).

A one-person home-based business is the simplest option for most job-trap escapees. Whether it is a sole proprietorship or is made "official" by taking the form of a corporation or limited liability company, it's a highly flexible option.

Recommended reading

"Should I Incorporate?" On the web at: www.turbotax.com/articles/ShouldIIncorporate.html.

"Should I Incorporate My Business?" On the web at: sbinfocanada.about.com/od/startup/f/incorporatebiz.htm. (Geared to Canadians; contains good general info and links.)

Tip: You do not have to incorporate in your own state. For small business startups, Wyoming may have the best U.S. incorporation laws. Nevada is also popular.

On the traditional end of the spectrum you'll find: Freelance art or writing; gardening or handyman work; child care; knitting, crocheting, sewing, or other forms of crafting; photography; accounting; baking; making jams and jellies; making soaps; producing honey, goat's milk, vegetables, or other farm products; pet grooming; legal services; counseling; sales (e.g. Avon, Amway); and more.

But with the Internet has come the ability to expand even a one-person business worldwide. (For instance, I have clients 2,000 miles away whom I have never met.) This has opened up many more possibilities. Consider:

- E-book publishing
- Screen printing and online sales of stickers, greeting cards, signs, etc.
- Consignment selling of other people's products (crafts, foods, etc.)
- Buying at garage sales and reselling on eBay
- Setting yourself up as a guru (a gift of gab can be more important than actual expertise)
- Making specialty products for niche markets (e.g. natural dyes; organic cosmetics; regional foods; regional or ethnic

craft items; gourmet pet foods; elegant babywear; custom gun-stocks)

- Even blogging — the ultimate hobby activity of keeping an online diary — has become a money-maker for a savvy few who collect donations, sell ads, and use their blogs to market products.

The best businesses begin with either a personal passion or a personal need. Take the case of Margy Brown, a rancher from the bleak, cold, windblown plains of Wyoming. Anybody who has ever spent much time in that nasty climate can tell you what Wyoming weather can do to your skin — dry it, turn it into a scaly mess, and crack it until it bleeds.

So Margy, at her kitchen table, began mixing beeswax, Aloe Vera, vitamins, and other ingredients — and the result became an entire line of skin-care products carrying her own "Cross A Ranch" brand. These pricey items now are well received in everyplace from tourist shops to feed stores.

A life-sustaining home-based business doesn't necessarily aim to remain small. Back in 1987, Karl Hess wrote about one company that aimed for both a good life for its participants and a larger scale:

> As with many other home businesses, Deva didn't start with a business plan but with a personal plan. The people who started it set as their first goal doing work which could be done in a home setting and which would keep their families together. ...They decided on clothing because much of the work, the actual sewing, could be done by other people in their own homes.[1]

Today, if you pop onto the Internet and go to www.devalifewear.com, you'll still see this family-oriented,

---

[1] Hess, Karl. *Capitalism for Kids.* Enterprise Publishing, Inc., Wilmington, DE, 1987. pp. 70-71.

lifestyle-conscious company, Deva Life Wear, selling comfortable hand-made clothing made from natural fibers like cotton and hemp. Their business is worldwide — but has never departed from its humane and human roots.

The cost of setting up a home-based business is usually just a fraction of that required to establish a store or other non-home business. But it can still require an enormous amount of administrative work and can entail risk. (Every job escapee who opts for self-employment has to face the potential dilemma of working even harder at independence than at job-holding.)

If you go independent you may not make as much as you did in the corporate world. But then, depending on your choice of occupation, your costs may be lower, as well. You might be able to save thousands every year on anything from taxes to the cost of commuting.

And when you love what you do and do it well you may find that you actually make more while feeling a lot less stressed and harried.

Collaborative community or neighborhood ventures

Although not the easiest option, forming (or joining) a community-based cooperative venture can be among the most satisfying choices. Such ventures not only offer income and interesting work for you, but can boost the health of your community and help neighborhoods regain control of their own economic future.

To learn more about this option, read Karl Hess' book *Community Technology* (available from Loompanics), in which he discusses the reasons, problems, and rewards of establishing a community-based aquaculture business in an urban area.

Such a business may begin with basically altruistic or social intentions. But the best community businesses may end up both profit-making *and* community-boosting.

Consider the case of Chugwater Chili, as explained on that spicy product's web site:

> Chugwater Chili Corporation came to being in June of 1986, when five farm and ranch families purchased the Wyoming State Championship Chili Recipe and turned it into a "for-profit" business to help the business community of the town of Chugwater. From humble beginnings in a home basement for an office and a ranch bunkhouse for packaging, the Corporation is now located at 210 1st Street, Chugwater, Wyoming. As our billboards along the highway suggests, we welcome visitors to stop in for a free taste of our products as well as to say hello.[2]

Before chili, the town of Chugwater was just a dying little spot whose only claim to fame was some pretty bluffs. But this single product put Chugwater on the food map of the Rocky Mountain states. Chugwater Chili is now known all over the region and is sold in grocery stores, as well as its own headquarters store.

I've deliberately used two examples from Wyoming — Cross A Ranch skin care products and Chugwater Chili — partly because Wyoming is considered one of the most difficult places in the country to earn a living. The entire state (one of the largest in the nation in square miles) has a smaller population than many cities — less than half a million people. The weather (and road conditions) are often hellacious. Distances between suppliers and customers are so vast many conventional businesses simply throw up their hands and don't even consider trying.

---

[2] http://www.chugwaterchili.com/aboutus.html

But those who think *unconventionally*, like Margy Brown and the ranch families who made Chugwater Chili a success, can fill niches that larger, more hidebound businesses won't touch. And therein lies one key to a successful community-based or home-based business.

Contracting with an employer

But not everyone needs — or wants — to venture completely out on their own. What if you were able to continue doing the job you do today — whether it be as a file clerk, physician, printing press operator, or teacher — but you were able to negotiate customized terms with your existing employer?

Rather than having to work a standardized 40-hour work week, you could negotiate a schedule that worked best for all parties. Say, you'd work 20 hours a week for three weeks out of the month, but 45 hours during the one week your boss regularly had more business volume. You'd get more time off. Your boss would only have to pay for the services she really needed. And everybody would have what suited them.

You'd be an independent contractor, which would mean you'd be responsible for supplying your own "benefits." But because she wouldn't have to endure all the paperwork, pay administrative costs of a benefit package, or make the employer's portion of your social security payment, your boss (now your client) could offer you higher pay. You'd be in charge of your own work and financial life. You could band together with other self-employed people to purchase group insurance policies that suited you, rather than having to accept the one-size-fits-all HMO plan your employer might offer. (Or these days, which your employer might not be able to afford to offer.)

You'd be your own boss, even while working for your old boss. And since you'd be self-employed, you'd not only receive higher pay, you'd also be able to use the IRS's Schedule C when filing your taxes — and Schedule C is the best thing that ever happened to any tax serf. Use your Schedule C self-employment write-offs well and you can keep more of your own money than most wage earners ever manage.

Sounds pretty good, doesn't it? Unfortunately, there's a catch. While it is possible under certain conditions to contract with a business that might otherwise hire you as an employee, the Internal Revenue Service absolutely hates the freedom of the contracting option. For more than 35 years, the IRS has been on the warpath against contracting.

The IRS knows contracting is too beneficial both to small employers and to workers who want more freedom and flexibility. They know it gives individuals more potential tax write-offs and makes it harder to collect taxes (because the employer doesn't remove taxes from week-to-week). So they constantly rule that contractual relationships are actually employer-employee relationships and they punish employers who try to give their workers this form of freedom and independence.

The IRS has ruled that if you work on a business' premises, if you contract only to one business, and if you're paid by the hour (for instance), you are an employee, even if you and those you work with have agreed otherwise. The government's main criterion for determining who is an employee is *whether the company directly controls what you do and how you do it.* You're somewhat at the IRS's mercy when it comes to determining that issue of "control."

Recommended reading

If you're considering becoming an independent contractor, you might want to first make sure the IRS isn't likely to swoop in at some later date and punish your clients by claiming they must treat you as an employee.

See the IRS publication "Independent Contractors vs. Employees" on the web at: www.irs.gov/businesses/small/article/0,,id=99921,00.html.

Dreary as this publication is, knowing its provisions might also help you talk your current employer into agreeing to change your relationship so you can have more independence and flexibility.

There are still ways to be an independent contractor in circumstances where you'd normally be an employee. For example, if you work on a business' premises, but you're paid based on completion of a specific task (and you set the terms of completing that task for yourself) the IRS may consider you an independent contractor. If you work off-premises or if you contract to more than one firm, the IRS is more likely to accept that you are a contractor.

You should not have to satisfy the IRS. Every adult should be able to contract voluntarily with other adults to provide peaceable, useful services as you see fit. But the taxman with his millions of incomprehensible words of rules and regulations is a reality we must all deal with.

The society which scorns excellence in plumbing because plumbing is a humble activity, and tolerates shoddiness in philosophy because philosophy is an exalted activity, will have neither good plumbing nor good phi-

losophy. Neither its pipes nor its theories will hold water. — John W. Gardner

Quitting work altogether and living off investments

Don't disregard this option just because you're not a millionaire! "Living off investments" sounds like something that only trust-fund babies and savvy stock market players can do. But in their book, *Your Money or Your Life,* Vicki Robin and Joe Dominguez explain how even people of very modest means can work toward that goal. They personally achieved that goal by both simplifying their needs and holding a relatively modest portfolio. At the time they wrote the book (in the early 1990s, shortly before Dominguez's death), they were living in a major American city on just $600 per month, most of which came from interest.

As I write this, interest rates are lower than they were then, which makes the prospect of investment-only living more problematic.

Nevertheless, consider: Let's say that in the future life you desire, you plan to be out of debt, to pay less in taxes, and to live in a part of the country where real estate prices are lower than where you currently live. You project that you can live perfectly well (though certainly not extravagantly) on $1,000 per month. You sell your home and walk away with $120,000 in equity — not at all unreasonable, these days. If you invest the money from your home in something that earns you just 5 percent per year, you'll have $6,000 per year — which is half of what you require to live on.

How much freelance, home-based work would you have to do to earn the other half? Even if you set up as a semi-skilled self-employed laborer, you're going to make *at least* $10 per hour. And probably more. Here's how many hours you'd have to work to earn the rest of your modest living, if you needed to earn $6,000 per year:

$10 per hour	11.5 hours per week
$15 per hour	7.7 hours per week
$20 per hour	5.8 hours per week

In my area, virtually every gardener, lawn trimmer, self-employed carpenter, or independent caregiver makes an income somewhere in that range. And some make even more.

The IRS currently allows (I hate that term, "allows," but that's the way our government is these days) most homeowners to sell a primary residence and exclude up to $250,000 (for an individual, or $500,000 for a couple) from capital gains taxes. This exclusion used to apply only to older people and was a "once-in-a-lifetime" exclusion. But the exclusion is now for anyone who can meet certain simple criteria[3], and it can be used again and again. So you can usually invest the full amount from the sale of a home.

When it comes to living off investments, we must never forget that the U.S. government also taxes the interest you'll earn. But if your total gross income is $12,000 per year, you're probably liable for little or no tax, in any case.

If you have no home to sell or no retirement plan to draw from or stock or mutual fund portfolio to convert into living capital, then you're at a disadvantage. But again turn to *Your Money or Your Life*. Robin and Dominguez show you how to begin building assets out of even the most ordinary, or even unpromising, income.

---

[3] For details see the IRS publication at www.irs.gov/faqs/faq-kw140.html. The description I've given in this chapter is simplified and should not be relied on as tax advice.

Quitting work altogether while your spouse earns the living

Conventional wisdom and the media tell us that we can't survive these days if all the adult members of our household don't bring in an income. And so we leave our children in the hands of strangers for the sake — as we perceive it — of economic survival.

But quite often, when we add up *all* the figures, common wisdom and the media turn out to be wrong. More often than we're willing to believe, having two jobs in the household *costs* us, rather than profits us.

If you're in a two-parent, two-earner household, sit down and make a list of every cost associated with the lowest-earning job (or the job with the least long-term potential). Consider *everything*:

- Cost of extra vehicle used primarily for work.
- Cost of gasoline, maintenance, and insurance for that vehicle.
- Cost of tolls, parking fees, and other aspects of travel to job.
- Cost of clothing needed only because of job.
- Cost of meals eaten out because of being on the job site.
- Cost of meals eaten out because of exhaustion after work.
- Cost of day care for children.
- Gifts, pools, parties, etc. on the job site.
- Increased taxes paid because of the income from this job.
- Etc.

Add it up. Be honest and thorough. And if at the end you realize that you're either losing or gaining so little from the second job that it's not worthwhile, consider quitting.

I say *consider* quitting, rather than "just quit!" because of course you might still have reason to hold a job, even if it isn't truly sustaining to the family.

For instance, I've always been personally horrified by the thought of being economically dependent on another person and therefore unable to escape should the relationship turn sour.

These days, too, personal self-esteem often hinges on income-earning. And both women and men alike crave the challenges and stimulation of the work place, the joy of success in the world, and the status of climbing the corporate ladder. That variety of "job dependence" can under some circumstances be a highly toxic attitude. Or it can represent a healthy search for excellence. But if it's a reality in our lives, we need to consider it before we spring the job trap.

> *I only go to work on days that don't end in a 'y'.* — Robert Paul

Our society tends to value money-earning labor over non-money-earning labor. When one partner in a relationship controls all the money, power in the relationship can get quickly and painfully out of balance. If one partner works for money and the other doesn't, both partners have to make a conscious effort to maintain the respect due when they are "separate but equal."

But even given all the many good, personal reasons that both partners in a relationship might want to continue to work, the conventional wisdom that two incomes are needed for a sustainable modern family is still simply quite often wrong when you truly look at the numbers.

If I were one of two earners in a family whose children were spending most of their day in the custody of strangers, I'd ask myself whether the entire two-earner imperative wasn't, in reality, just one more unhealthy manifestation of the Job Culture. And I'd ask whether the government — with its increased tax revenues — wasn't making out like a bandit at the expense of me, my partner, and our children.

Before leaving this subject, I should add that the non-earning spouse by no means has to be the woman. In fact, when I think of the single-earner families in my circle of acquaintances, I note that most of the stay-at-homes are house*husbands*, not wives.

Finally, the true "traditional family" did not consist (as conservatives would have it) of a stay-at-home wife and a husband whose main job was to go away somewhere to earn money. The true traditional family consisted of both parents being at home with their children, often with the entire family working together in workshop, inn, or farm. And often with a large extended family and stable neighbor-community or tribe around to help. Again, such a life was far from perfect, but it was better balanced than what we've come to accept as "normal" and more emotionally healthy for all concerned than the psychological isolation chamber we erroneously consider a "traditional" family.

> *If you don't want to work you have to work to earn enough money so that you won't have to work.* — Ogden Nash

Telecommuting

We keep hearing from the media that telecommuting is an up-and-coming option — a godsend that will relieve job stress, cut down on freeway gridlock, and cure many other job ills.

The big promise remains so far unfulfilled because, even in fields like software engineering which require long periods of solo work, so many employers are simply afraid to let their workers out of their sight. They don't trust their workers to keep their promises or complete their assignments.

So telecommuting tends to be something employers allow once a week. Or under special circumstances (e.g. needing to be home with a sick child; needing a period of focused work to complete a specific project).

And, of course, there are still many fields where telecommuting simply isn't an option. Can't sling burgers or do a bank teller's job via telephone.

But increasingly, companies *are* allowing telecommuting for employees (or contractors) whose skills are so valuable they can set their own terms. Or to keep employees happy that they otherwise might fear losing.

Telecommuting in itself isn't a true escape from the job trap. But it can be a pressure-release valve. And once you persuade your employer that you work well on your own, telecommuting has the potential to lead in several interesting directions. (Don't forget that working off-premises is one of the IRS's criteria for determining who's "allowed" to be an independent contractor, if that's the way you choose to go.)

Job sharing

Job sharing is another allegedly sanity-producing option once much-touted by the media. Job sharing was going to allow individuals to spend more time with their families, lead to more flexible hours, and offer a dozen other benefits.

But the complications of "allowing" two people to inhabit one job are seriously daunting, both to the sharers and to HR departments (and sometimes to bosses and co-workers). So this is an option that's never truly taken off. Nevertheless, it can be a worthwhile option if you're a creative thinker working in an environment where creativity and flexibility are welcomed.

Job sharing requires initiative on your part. It isn't simply a matter of two people working part-time to fulfill one function. Job sharing begins with you finding a potential partner who's willing and able to do the same work you do. This might be someone already in your company or someone outside.

You two find each other. You two work out the details. Then you make a proposal to your boss, complete with details on how the job share would work. (For instance, how would the sharers share information so that responsibilities would never get dropped or questions go unanswered?)

Recommended reading

"What is Job Sharing?" On the web at:

www.ivillage.co.uk/workcareer/worklife/flexwork/articles/0,,202_156231,00.html. (Geared to a British audience, but contains good general information.)

"Job Sharing Proposal Strategy" On the web at: www.workoptions.com/jobshare.htm.

Temp work

Then there is the time-honored option of temp work, which has so long been a blessing to the unemployed, to students, to workers who don't stay long in one area, to people who just need to pick up a few extra dollars now and then, and to companies with seasonal or otherwise short-term needs for extra workers.

Temp work can encompass anything from data entry during inventory or tax season to adventure jobs in parks during recreation seasons.

Temp work often leads to long-term employment, with companies hiring temps who've proved themselves competent, thus bypassing the risk of hiring strangers. Temp work can also actually *be* long-term work; temp agencies usually handle all the messy payroll details for the workers, and some companies enjoy the relief of not having to deal with that. (There've been some government crackdowns on the practice of "long-term temp" work, however.)

Recommended reading

"Temp Work Can Have Permanent Benefits" by Peter Vogt. An overview article directed toward people newly entering the work force. On the web at: content.monstertrak.monster.com/resources/archive/onthejob/tempwork/.

"The Temp Workers Guide to Self-Fulfillment" by Dennis Fiery. A highly attitudinal and sometimes profane article about making temp work benefit you. On the web at: www.loompanics.com/Articles/Temp.htm.

Part-time work (a misnomer)

Finally, you might want to explore the option of traditional part-time work.

"Part-time" is really a Job Culture misnomer. All work in a balanced life is "part-time." To work "full-time" is inherently a very out-of-balance thing.

But alas, it's another Job Culture reality that "part-time" work often carries with it lower pay and fewer valuable benefits than 40+ hour a week servitude. Part-time work has too long been the option of less skilled, and less career-oriented workers, so it's gotten a bad reputation and carries with it a lot of baggage it really ought not have to carry.

I list it last because it's the least creative, and in many ways the least rewarding, of all ways to gain balance between work and other aspects of life. When you work part-time, you remain an employee, rather than an independent. And you usually receive proportionally less than people who do exactly the same work but do it for longer hours.

> *The trouble with unemployment is that the minute you wake up in the morning you're on the job.* — Slappy White

Nevertheless, part-time work doesn't require you to challenge "the system" (as job-sharing or telecommuting might). It doesn't put your own money at risk (as self-employment might). And opportunities for it are everywhere, from small towns to big cities.

Going from "full-time" to "part-time" can also be part of a long-term exit strategy from the job trap and the Job Culture. You can work part-time while training yourself for a more gratifying career. Working part-time can give you opportunity to homeschool your children. To build a business on the side. To write a book. To research your future choices. So I list it here as one more option, even though it's part of the traditional Job Culture.

Because after all, options is what this chapter is about.

Now, in the next chapter let's look outside the job world, at some of the other changes you might make in your life that will enable you to live on less, be more financially flexible, or whatever else it will take to make your particular escape from the job trap successful.

When your goal seems impossibly big ...

Take a single small step.

Small steps can sometimes carry you unexpected distances. Let's say, for instance, that on your way toward your new workstyle goal, you want to reduce expenses. You could also stand to lose a little weight and get in better condition.

So to save just a tiny bit on gas and to reduce parking fees, you begin parking a mile from work three days a week and walking the rest of the way.

You quickly discover that the walk, in addition to helping lighten both your budget and your body, serves as a reminder of the kind of peaceful, uninterrupted activity you hope to achieve after you spring the job trap. So the walk becomes a motivator, keeping you on track.

You also discover that creative ideas flow freely while you walk. Your mind wraps itself playfully around ideas. Letting your spirit soar, you're struck repeatedly by insights that help you surmount obstacles that once seemed beyond your ability to overcome.

One day perhaps you even see some little thing in a store window or on the lawn of a house that gives you an idea for something you could make or do. It's something you'd never in the world have noticed, had you been in your vehicle, isolated from your surroundings and focused on traffic.

And so the seemingly tiny step of walking a mile to your job becomes a huge advance along your path.

Chapter Six
Practical Steps

I'm not going to attempt to offer a well-ordered, step-by-step list of actions you should take in seeking a more balanced, more free work life. Because as we've touched on earlier, everyone approaches the journey differently.

Those who are organized and linear will quickly make their own list of steps and stages without prompting from any writer.

Those who are more non-linear and serendipitous in their approach to life will either blithely ignore anyone else's step-by-step recommendations or (much worse) will try to follow them, find the process absurd, and either become angry at themselves or at yours truly for failing to be good at the list game.

The impulse-driven might simply wake up one day and say, "Screw it, I'm outta here," then dance off into the unknown without planning.

Those who are discontent but don't really want to change would simply sit and find fault with anything anyone else suggested — then go on perversely enjoying being stuck and complaining about it.

Others might suddenly find change thrust upon them by circumstances beyond their control — a layoff, a bankruptcy, illness, or accident — and have to tap-dance their way into the altered future, heedless of anyone's recommendations.

And all that's as it should be. Because after all, one of the big problems with the Job Culture is that it's squeezed too many millions of individuals in to one-size-fits-all (or rather one-size-doesn't-fit-all) structures.

If you're a square peg, you shouldn't have to fit into any pre-determined round hole! *You* are the only living expert in your own life. Part of the process of self-liberation is accepting, then reveling in, your power to change what can be changed. And to change it *in your own way*.

The most helpful thing any outsider can do is offer suggestions — tips, guidelines, bright ideas — to apply to your own situation in your own way. So ...on with it.

Twelve Tips for Springing the Job Trap

1. Don't wait for the world to change.
2. Know what you want.
3. Reduce debt.
4. Reduce expenses.
5. Involve your partner and dependents (but not necessarily the rest of your family).
6. Don't just change your job, change your self.
7. Learn to say no.
8. Build alternative skills and interests.
9. Be flexible and creative.
10. Don't be afraid to screw up.
11. Don't burn your bridges.

12. Do it for love.

1. Don't wait for the world to change.

Our task, here and now, is not to change the entire Job Culture, but to attain as much balance, satisfaction, and freedom in work as we can attain *for ourselves* no matter what the external circumstances. If we wait for somebody else to change — our employers, politicians, disapproving relatives, etc. — we'll have a handy, lifelong excuse for doing absolutely nothing to make our lives happier.

Acknowledge that the world will throw some obstacles in your path. Some of those obstacles you might be able to lever out of your way, others you'll have to route around. Some, you might just have to live with. But if you allow all those obstacles to stop you completely, then you might rightly ask yourself if *you* could actually be the biggest obstacle in your own path.

Keep this uppermost in mind: *Whatever* the problems and restrictions, there is *always* something you can do to move toward your dream. At times, it may be a very small something. You may wonder if the step is even worth taking. But small steps are still worth taking. And you never know when a small step will lead you to a place where you can take a big jump.

> *Kill my boss? Do I dare live out the American dream?*
> — Homer Simpson

2. Know what you want.

That's what all of Chapter Four was about. I mention it here, in this list of "practical steps," for one reason: to say that when it comes to making major life changes, sometimes the most dreamy, abstract, visionary, speculative things we do are *practical*.

The more vividly you envision *living* in the free, satisfying future you hope for, the more inspired you'll be to stay on course and to take the actions that'll get you to your goal even when the present looks tough.

3. Reduce debt.

If you plan to exit the job trap and immediately go on to something bigger and better, more power to you. In that case, assuming you have real prospects of instantly improved prosperity, you don't have to worry about lowering your debt.

Or perhaps you're one of the smart or lucky people who hasn't run up a lot of debt in the first place.

But for most people in these credit-mad days, debt is the biggest, strongest chain that binds a body to a job and the Job Culture.

As I write this, Americans have followed their government on a mad spending spree — taking every dime of equity out of their homes to finance cars and vacations and other things of little lasting value, running up credit cards as though life were one big party for which the bills were never going to come due.

The further we get into the debt habit, the more dependent we become. On banks. On jobs. On the usurers of the credit-card industry.

Getting out can be hard — and might look darned near impossible when we're just starting. It might help to remember what debt is:

Debt is the act of selling our future for some benefit today.

When we go into debt, we're selling ourselves into bondage. We are agreeing to give some amount of our future labor, time, and *life* to somebody in exchange for getting something today.

Yuch! Who wants to do that, unless they really *have* to? Yet it's so easy to do when we don't think too hard about the real meaning and consequences of debt.

Debt has valid uses. Borrowing to start a business or buy an asset whose value is likely to appreciate gives you leverage from which you can make future profits — profits that exceed the cost of the debt. A student loan might help you buy a higher future income. But borrowing simply to *buy stuff* is not wise.

Once again, however, we find ourselves in the familiar situation where the Job Culture has landed us in a mix of benefits and drawbacks.

For instance: The wonders of the Industrial Revolution brought us automobiles everyone could afford. Great! Soon, our jobs and needed services were further and further from home so that most of us *had* to have motor vehicles. Well, okay, cars were affordable for many years. Now the wonders of the post-industrial revolution (coupled with government regulatory requirements on vehicle design) bring us increasingly sophisticated vehicles that we can afford *only if we sell ourselves into debt slavery*. That's nuts!

Credit-card debt: A painless way out

Paying off mountains of credit-card debt can seem like an insurmountable task. Here's a relatively painless way of doing it. I'm not sure who first came up with this method; it's been around a long time. But I am sure that it works.

1. Stop charging on the card.
2. Instead of making a payment once a month, pay *one half* of the minimum payment every two weeks.
3. Then continue to pay that same amount every two weeks until the card is paid off.

This method has several advantages. First, by making 26 biweekly payments, you're making the equivalent of 13, not the standard 12, monthly payments.

By paying one-half of the required payment earlier in the month, you're also routinely cutting down on the interest the lender is piling up against your account.

By continuing to make the same payment even when the lender drops the required minimum, you're causing yourself no pain — but depriving the lender of a steadily increasing amount of interest.

Just two things to look out for: First, be sure there are no penalties for early payoff (with credit cards, there seldom are). Second, when you begin this plan, make your first biweekly payment immediately after you receive the bill. You *must* make sure that the full monthly minimum reaches the lender before the due date, or they'll hit you with interest penalties. Once you've gotten on your schedule, though, it's free sailing.

All kinds of experts will tell you how to get out of debt. Unfortunately, a lot of the advice is self-serving (e.g. from debt-counseling services whose aim is to make money off your desperation) and a lot of advice just might not fit your circumstances or your psychology.

Here are two really good, reliable sources for getting out of debt, each one geared to different needs:

The Motley Fool How-To Guide: How To Get Out of Debt
www.fool.com/seminars/sp/index.htm?sid=0001&lid=000&pid=0000

The Motley Fool is an online financial-management and investment guide that combines sensible advice with an irreverent attitude. Its guide to getting out of debt begins with some basic definitions — like the difference between "good" debt and "bad" debt — and some eye-opening info on the real impact of credit-card debt in our lives. As you begin this brief five-step online course, you download a friendly 20-page workbook you can use to analyze your personal debt picture and work out your personal solutions with the wise Fool's help. The Fool offers fairly conventional advice — sound, but familiar to anybody who's been down the debt road.

For some of us, a more unconventional approach is called for:

Your Money or Your Life:
Transforming Your Relationship with Money
and Achieving Financial Independence
by Vicki Robin and Joe Dominguez

I've made this recommendation probably a dozen times in the last eight years. (I've already made it in this book, in fact.) *Your Money or Your Life* isn't for everyone. Its authors were early adherents of the so-called voluntary simplicity movement, and their advice is not geared to people who want to remain in the traditional Job-and-Debt Culture. But then, you don't want to stay in that trap, either, do you? So even if you disagree with parts of their philosophy (as I do) let Robin and Dominguez guide you through a process that teaches you a whole new relationship to money. This is not a book about budgeting. It's not about scrimping, saving, or sacrificing. It's about changing the way you view spending — then changing your actions in productive, even joyful ways. You might find, after following the authors' methods, that you actually spend more in certain areas of your life — because you choose to put more into those areas even while changing your bad spending habits overall.

4. Reduce expenses.

Reducing expenses goes hand-in-hand with getting out of debt. Again, if you're moving from a prosperous job to a prosperous non-job, no worry. Spend away!

But for the rest of us, moving from "secure" employment to some less life-consuming alternative entails risk, and the more financial flexibility we can grant ourselves, the better.

As you get out of debt, you're automatically reducing many monthly expenses — perhaps even reducing some very big ones (those high-interest credit-card bills, car loans, and other whopping monthly bills). But along with that, look around and see what else you can do. Be aware of what you're spending cash-money on (the methods Robin and Dominguez recommend can help here, too, every day). Then see where you can painlessly spend less.

- Buying a latte every day? Have you considered you might be spending as much as $100 per month, just slurping those Starbucks?
- Could you get by just as well with a less expensive car?
- Could you bike to work or to the store?
- A home-cooked dinner and a DVD rental with friends might be just as much fun as that $100+ night on the town.
- How many phone lines does one family really need?
- If you live in one of the corners of the country with soaring real estate prices, could you move elsewhere — and use the money from the sale of your house to finance a new work venture? Or use your equity on that yuppie palace to pay cash for a home in Kansas or rural New Mexico?
- The latest, greatest electronic toy might really not add as much to your life as you used to think.

- If you moved to a non-job, you might end up saving on items like suits, pantyhose, ties, restaurant lunches, gasoline, entries in the office football pool, gifts for co-workers you scarcely even know, and impulse purchases made while seeking “recreation.”
- And you can probably think of a dozen other places to cut expenses in your own life, before, during, and after you make your personal transition.

The object here isn’t to surrender all prosperity. It’s to give yourself room to maneuver so that you don’t have to go racing straight back into the job trap if your workstyle changes don’t immediately work out. Besides that, after you’ve made your workstyle transition and started to eliminate some of your primarily job-driven expenses, you’ll have more to spend on the things you really enjoy.

For instance, your new non-job might lead to a huge reduction in income taxes (either because you make less or because you’ve launched a new entrepreneurial venture that enables you to take more tax write-offs). And just think what a positive impact *that* reduction in spending could have on your life and your future! Reducing spending isn’t all about painful sacrifice.

> *I slip from workaholic to bum real easy.* — Matthew Broderick

5. Involve your partner and dependents.

This ought to go without saying. If you have children or a partner, include them into your planning as early as possible.

Find out whether your partner shares your goals or aspirations — or might have complementary aspirations. If your partner wants to head in a similar direction — or is willing to support you as you go — what joy! On the other hand, if your partner is threatened by your desire for change (it happens, alas) or dislikes your ideas for some other reason ...better to know that early on. You might need to put your powers of persuasion to work. Or start making alternate plans.

Children, depending on their ages and temperaments, might come into the planning later than your spouse or significant other. But they'll also cope better if they feel they've had some part in the decision-making. After all, lifestyle and workstyle changes are often *about* your children, in a sense. About the desire to share more of life with them, to take more responsibility and more joy in their upbringing. To share the satisfaction of meaningful work with them.

And sometimes the kids will surprise you. Recently, a friend made drastic workstyle and lifestyle changes. The changes took him away from a full-time job in a major city to precarious self-employment 10 miles off-grid. You couldn't have much more of a change than that! And as it happened, he and his family made thc change almost overnight, without the years of planning they'd anticipated.

He and his wife had originally figured to make the move only after their teenage daughter was out of school and on her own. In the months of scrambling to sell their urban house, get a well dug, design a solar system, etc., they initially assumed their daughter would want to stay behind with relatives in the city to be with her old friends and enjoy "civilization." But once they talked about it, it turned out that the daughter was more than ready for the adventure of off-grid life, even if it meant giving up much that seemed to matter to her.

Talking early and openly was a good idea and it took one burden off this overburdened life-changer.

On the other hand, it might *not* be a good idea to involve extended family members in your workstyle and lifestyle planning. Those people who aren't going to come directly along with you on your future journey might have agendas for you that your heart doesn't share, and that can only add conflict, guilt, and remorse — baggage you don't need to carry.

> *There's a time when you have to separate yourself from what other people expect of you, and do what you love. Because if you find yourself 50 years old and you aren't doing what you love, then what's the point?* — Jim Carrey

I'll never forget, when I walked out of my "exciting" job, the sneering criticism of one of my closest relatives. Like me, this woman came out of working-class roots and eventually rose into something better. But unlike me, she learned to cherish luxury cars, urban townhouses, antiques, and first-class travel.

She was certain I'd eventually come to my senses and return to *her* idea of the good life. But in the meantime, she let me and everyone around us know how foolish I was for "giving up the fast lane for a rickety playhouse overlooking Walden Puddle."

Such judgments can hurt. And when they come in the form of well-intentioned "good advice" while you're trying to make decisions about your own life, they can be very destructive. "For your own good" is an excuse that loving, but insecure, controlling people will use to hold you back.

Those who are on your journey with you deserve to be consulted. Those who are only standing beside your path watching shouldn't be allowed to deter you.

6. Don't *merely* change your job. Change your self.

If your only problem with your job is that you're bored out of your mind or that a particular manager has a personality conflict with you, then perhaps you can solve your most immediate job-trap problem just by leaving that position.

But sometimes we'll escape a job, only to find that we bring the real problem with us. Because the real problem may be within us.

I speak from personal experience. My workstyle (described in Chapter Four) sounds heavenly. And it should be.

But that's before you factor in my own tendency to make things difficult. Let me count the ways! Or let me not, because the list of all my self-caused work problems would bore you. Suffice to say that, even though I don't require all that many billable hours a week to survive, my tendency to 1) goof off and postpone everything till the last minute and 2) get myself into positions where clients dump more work on me than I want causes me to often end up working seven days a week and feeling pressured and frenzied. I also have the attention span of a five-year-old on speed, which doesn't help. I must force myself to focus when every ring of the telephone, nudge of a dog's nose, or even a dirty dish sitting quietly in the sink can pull my attention away from what I ought to be doing.

I love what I do. But merely being out of the world of conventional job-jobs doesn't mean all my problems are solved! I might need meditation to help me calm and focus. I might need to impose more structure on my work days so the work will stay within certain time boundaries. I might even need — I hate even to utter the word — discipline.

Going from a conventional job into an alternative workstyle will *always* require some adjustment, and it's hard to predict in advance what adjustments we'll personally require.

Point to ponder

If you achieve major goals and find that you're still unhappy, stop and ask why. Even more important, look within yourself. Chances are, the real problem lies in an attitude or a set of assumptions you've carried along the road with you — an attitude you might do better to shed.

Sometimes we get into rush-rush habits that don't actually serve us well, but that we've allowed to become part of the fabric of our workstyle. Sometimes we have personality problems that we bring to every encounter; we always blame the other guy, of course. But folks who encounter similar problems in job after job need to ask themselves how much of the problem lies in the job world and how much comes from their own attitudes or ways of doing things. Worriers will continue to worry, wherever they are. Chronically late folk will continue to have problems delivering on time (and that can cause even *more* problems to the self-employed than to the employed).

On the plus side, we may also need to learn to give ourselves permission to be happy. Some of us have gotten so used to the idea that work has to be ...well, work, that we can't quite believe that it's really okay to take pleasure in it.

7. Learn to say no.

One of the ways we can get more pleasure from our work and decrease the dominance of odious responsibilities in our lives is to *learn to say no*. This is particularly important after we've already resolved to change our work styles to make job-work less all-consuming.

You want me to handle a rush project over the weekend when I've got other plans? *No.*

You want me to take on an entirely new set of responsibilities that don't fit my vision for my future? *No.*

You want me to break my concentration on something important so I can pay attention to something less important? *No.*

You want me to do free work, with ardent promises that it'll lead to vast opportunities later? *Not unless you can show me some real potential*. (Most people asking for freebies will *always* ask for freebies.)

Learning to say no is a subset of changing oneself. It can be *very, very hard*, especially if you're a people pleaser. Or if you're starting up a new business and you don't want to turn away work. Quite often, we say *yes* out of habit. Or out of fear.

And of course, there are times we *should* say yes to a change of plans, if that yes might lead to interesting new opportunities. Or if it might help us toward a specific, short-term financial goal.

But saying *yes* to what everyone else wants all the time means we're always deferring what *we* want. And that's no way to build a harmonious life.

We need to learn to give a big, enthusiastic *yes* to what furthers our balanced, satisfying work life and to say no to most things that distract from our goal.

8. Build alternative skills and interests.

Author (and sailor, aviator, engineer, physicist, inventor, etc.) Robert Heinlein wrote: "A human being should be able to change a diaper, plan an invasion, butcher a hog, conn a ship, design a building, write a sonnet, balance accounts, build a wall, set a bone, comfort the dying, take orders, give orders, cooperate, act alone, solve equations, analyze a new problem, pitch manure, program a computer, cook a tasty meal, fight efficiently, die gallantly. Specialization is for insects."

While Heinlein's list may be daunting, the basic truth is in there for anyone seeking a more well-rounded life. The Job Culture and the post-Industrial Revolution have imposed specialization on us — not because we human beings are better off, *qua* human beings, by becoming specialists. But because production of goods and delivery of services in the complex Job Culture requires specialization.

Unless we are driven to specialize because we have a grand passion, specialization 40 hours or more a week is simply another form of serving the machine. Of course, it's another case in which serving the machine brings us economic and other benefits. Specialists are often paid more highly than generalists. And generalists may not even get hired at all, since Human Resource bureaucrats don't know what slot to file them in. But specializing on the job, unless it fulfills our passion, is still serving the machine and not serving the primary needs of our everyday lives.

> *The easiest job in the world has to be coroner. Surgery on dead people. What's the worst thing that could happen? If everything went wrong, maybe you'd get a pulse.* — Dennis Miller

Approximately one quarter of all Americans who retire return to some sort of job within a year — not because they're economically driven to, but simply because they're bored out of their minds! Imagine it. Millions of people spend 40 hours a week, busy and engaged, but the moment they're free to pursue their own interests, they discover they don't really *have* any interests.

If that's not the saddest commentary on what the Job Culture has done to us, then I don't know what is.

Life is filled with skills to learn, places to see, projects to undertake, causes needing volunteers, people to enjoy, questions to be explored — or just plain beauty to contemplate. Yet these people know nothing except trudging to work and they feel useless and bored without a job as their life's driver.

Never forget that humans first rose above the other animals *not* because we specialized, but precisely because we didn't. *They* had more impressive teeth or claws or fur or armor or the ability to change colors and become invisible. *We* had and should still have, the ability to do many things.

A now-famous study (called the "nun study" because the subjects were aged members of the School Sisters of Notre Dame in Mankato, Minnesota) examined the consequences of aging on the human brain. Until this long-term study was conducted, the assumption had been widely held that the human brain simply wore out over time — thus the susceptibility of the aged to Alzheimer's.

But the nun study showed something remarkable — that people whose minds continued to be stimulated and challenged showed far fewer effects of Alzheimer's — *even when autopsies later revealed that they had the disease*. In particular, learning new things and having new experiences was found to keep the brain alive and growing. Even as Alzheimer's ate holes in the brain, new brain tissue was forming around the damaged areas in the brains of those who actively pursued learning.

Those who simply sat in front of a TV set, on the other hand — those who stopped challenging themselves — showed far more symptoms of Alzheimer's.

Now perhaps you're only twentysomething or thirtysomething as you read this. You're hardly worried about Alzheimer's. But the meaning of the nun study goes far beyond a bunch of old ladies.

Just as our bodies get healthier with exercise, so do our brains. Learning and doing new things is a way to maximize your potential for better human health. And when you have freed yourself from a 40-hour a week trap of monotonous specialization, you'll have more opportunities to exercise the most important "muscle" you've got.

Creating structure

One of the biggest problems for people who retire or who otherwise seek a more leisurely life is lack of structure. When we don't have to leap out of bed at the sound of the alarm clock or hit the office exactly at 8:30, we often find ourselves doing *nothing*. Or just piddling around with meaningless tasks — surfing the Net, cleaning dust bunnies from under the bed, chatting on the phone, roaming the mall.

Even if you're obligated to earn a living, when you're not driven by structure or deadlines, it's easy (as I know all too well) to discover that half the day has passed and you've done nothing. And now you don't feel like doing anything, either.

You can create structure for yourself in many ways, depending on your personal style. Some possibilities:

- Start out every day by taking a long walk with the dog immediately after breakfast. The moment you come back to the house, you'll get down to your serious work.
- Assign deadlines to your projects even when they don't have any.
- Play a regularly scheduled competitive sport. This keeps you in the habit of keeping time commitments and keeps your mind and body sharp.
- Have an area of your house that is strictly your workspace — with no distractions in it. Go in there and close the door when it's time to work.
- Turn off the phone, yank the wireless network card out of your computer or whatever else you need to do to keep distractions to a minimum.

9. Be flexible and creative.

In one sense, this point is a corollary of Point 8. Being flexible and creative is healthier — and will make you happier — than being rigidly locked into routine.

But we're talking *practical* steps here. And when you're leaving the job trap for new life ventures, flexibility and creativity are useful career skills.

It takes creativity even to envision springing the trap. Creativity can also help you craft custom forms of escape, such as job sharing or independent contracting.

Flexibility may be required to make your escape a success. You might, for instance, leave your job to start a table-top business, only to find that there's no apparent demand for your service. With rigid thinking, your new life could whither away right there.

With a creative mind and a willingness to explore options, on the other hand, you can figure out how better to market your service. Or you might find unexpected outlets for your product. Or, if you really need to, figure out another home-based business you can swing right into so you don't have to run back to your employer's cage.

10. Don't be afraid to screw up.

What if you made a product that didn't work the way you intended? Let's say it was a glue that just plain wasn't sticky enough. Everybody knows that when you glue something it's supposed to stay put permanently, right? (Unless you attack the glue with a solvent.) So a glue that's only lightly, temporarily sticky must really be a dud.

Until somebody gets the idea to make Post-It Notes with it. In which case it becomes one of the world's most successful products.

This is, of course, one of many stories of failures that either became, or indirectly led to, great successes in business.

We fear to screw up for so many reasons. Because we don't want others to laugh at us. Because we don't want to face a failure in the mirror. Because we're competitive. Because failure could put us in the poorhouse.

All very true. But when you escape the job trap ...when you reduce your debt and your monthly bills ...when you reduce your discretionary spending ...when earning a living becomes a *part* of your life, but no longer the desperately vital center of your life ...you can afford to experiment. You can afford to take risks. You can afford to make mistakes on the road to your better life.

When you live life more creatively, you will make mistakes. Mistakes — sometimes even grand and glorious screw-ups — are part of the creative process.

You can be safe and never take risks. But then, if you were really of that mindset, you wouldn't be reading this book, would you?

How to keep from working

A couple of pages ago, we looked at a few ways to motivate yourself to work when you have no inherent schedule or deadlines. But many of us also have a related problem: the inability to *stop* working when we really ought to be taking it easy or enjoying other parts of our lives.

If you find your work stretching out beyond all reason ...

- Set fixed hours in which you'll work. Then stop when those hours end. Resist the temptation to take care of "just one more little thing."
- Don't answer business calls except during business hours.
- Schedule regular (and leisurely) lunches or coffee gatherings with friends — and always make a point of being there.
- Train yourself not to procrastinate. A lot of overwork has less to do with productivity than with *lack* of productivity.
- Schedule a regular daily playtime with the dog or the kids. Don't postpone or cancel it unless the sky is falling.
- Set aside a special work area — then never enter that area except to do defined work.

11. Don't burn your bridges.

Sometimes the best resource for your new life comes from your old life.

In my adult life I've held three "job-jobs" — one because it sounded so exciting I allowed myself to be seduced out of my independence, two others because I needed a solid base for a short time after moving to a new area. From each job, I gained something valuable. And in each case, one of the prime values was that I gained a client for my freelance work.

I had such a good relationship with each of these employers that when I left them (simply because I ultimately preferred my independence and disliked the artificial schedules and conventions of the job world) the former employers continued to hire me — sometimes only for a few months, sometimes for several years — to do freelance work for them.

After I returned to freelancing I had the best of both worlds, Job Culture contacts and personal freedom.

Even if there's no potential for continuing to work independently for your former employer after you spring the job trap, keeping a great relationship is still a good idea. What if you experience a setback and need to return temporarily to the conventional job fold? What if you need a favorable reference? What if you need your former employer one day as a vendor to your own new business? What if you need to seek advice from an expert who works at your former firm?

For all these reasons — and for the simple joy of living in productive peace — it's always a good idea to maintain at least a cordial relationship with your former employer, manager, or co-workers. No matter how uneasy things are at work, don't go stomping off mad. Don't slam doors you may need to open in the future.

12. Do it for love.

Many business books (which this is not) will tell you to do careful market research before going into any independent venture. I assume many readers of this book *will* want to go independent.

There's wisdom in taking a careful, methodical approach. Before starting your own small business, it would be a good idea to read the book *Look Before You Leap: Market Research Made Easy,*[1] a very friendly and useful book for the brand-new entrepreneur on a budget.

Market research can help you identify your potential market, craft an advertising message designed to appeal to them, know which media your customers get their information from, and even help you understand the psychological ins and outs by which people might choose your product or service over another.

But too many advisers have raised market research to a holy status it doesn't deserve. We need look no further than the beverage cooler at the nearest grocery store for a prime example of that fact. In 1985, the Coca Cola Company — armed with millions of dollars of research that plainly showed that customers preferred the sharper, more "modern" taste of Pepsi, suddenly tossed out their century-old product and replaced it with "New Coke." New Coke was on the shelves just 79 days before Coca Cola was forced by a worldwide customer uprising and the scorching mockery of the media to bring back what they then called "Classic Coke."

Today, the lesson of New Coke — that marvel of market research — is taught in business schools, right along with Ford's ill-timed introduction of the Edsel, as one of the great marketing disasters of all time.

---

1 Doman, Don, et al. Self-Counsel Press, Vancouver, BC, Canada. http://www.publicdoman.com/Look.html

Point to ponder

If someone asks, "What do you do?," what's the first thing you say?

If you're like most people, you answer by stating your *job.* "I'm a printing pressman." "I'm a clerk at Wal-Mart." "I'm a painter." "I'm in sales."

Now, what if someone were to ask, "What do you like to do?"

Would you answer with your profession?

To a person springing the job trap and going into independent business, I would say this: Do your market research, sure. If your research and your gut tell you different things, first try to find some way to reconcile the two. But if dry research and your heart continue to conflict, go with your heart. When you're passionate about what you do or what you make, you'll be motivated to find a market for it, even where research warns you of dangers in your path.

Something similar holds true even if you're just switching from one type of employment to another. In the long run, doing what you love is more practical than doing what dry figures, studies, and "experts" tell you you should do.

All the market research in the world, all the expert advice, even all the financial success in the world will fail you if they don't lead to your own deeply held idea of personal happiness. Listen to the words of successful and satisfied attorney-author Butler Shaffer:

> Do the kind of work in which you enjoy the work as an end in itself. In other words ...discover the kind of work you would perform even if you did not get paid for it, or, even where you had to pay to perform it. After many years in which I worked with management — as a labor lawyer — I have come to the conclusion that work that is performed primarily for the purpose of making money — or deriving any

other side benefit (such as status, power, etc.) — will almost always drive the individual nuts (slowly or quickly).[2]

Once again, a seemingly vague, airy, indefinable step is among the most practical of all. When you love what you do, you're motivated to overcome obstacles. Motivated to plunge in every day. Motivated to rise to new heights. Motivated to link your love and your life into one harmonious, balanced whole.

And that is what ultimately lifts us out of the worst of the job trap.

Recommended reading

What Color Is Your Parachute?: A Practical Manual for Job-Hunters and Career-Changers by Richard Nelson Bolles, Ten Speed Press, Berkeley, CA, 2004.

What Color Is Your Parachute Workbook: How to Create a Picture of Your Ideal Job or Next Career by Richard Nelson Bolles, Ten Speed Press, Berkeley, CA, 1998.

---

2 Hess, Karl. *Capitalism for Kids.* Enterprise Publishing, Inc., Wilmington, DE, 1987. pp. 164-165.

Getting there

- Take small steps toward your goals when opportunities present themselves. Don't despair because the steps may seem too small to be useful.
- Take giant leaps toward your goals when opportunities present themselves. Just be sure the leaps are within your comfort limits for coping with risk.
- If you backslide, kick yourself in the butt. Then forgive yourself and go on.
- Keep your main goals actively in mind. Over time you'll discover that you've continued to move in the right direction, even when you didn't think you were making progress.
- Don't expect utopia. Even the most ideal life has its troubles. Rely on perspective and a sense of humor to help you enjoy what you've attained.

The #1 most important thing

Real estate mavens famously say that the three most important factors in their business are: "Location, location, and location."

The author Ayn Rand, when asked to name the three most important aspects of good fiction, answered: "Plot, plot, and plot."

When you're springing the job trap, the three most important traits to take into your new life with you are: "Attitude, attitude, and attitude."

You can go through all the "correct" steps. You can make all the "correct" choices, according to the experts. But if you don't have the right attitude, you'll either fail or merely be unhappy with your outward success.

- Love what you do.
- Do it with passion.

- Determine that independence is more important than even the most attractive silver chains, even when independence seems difficult.
- Meet obstacles with the kind of creativity that can ultimately turn them into opportunities.

Part III
The Rest of the World

And then there is this kind of family: Development of the mind is prized for its own sake, the human mind being regarded as the supreme instrument of human action, the agency of human creativity, the definer and author of human progress. Work is prized as the process through which human minds react with the environment and transform parts of it to human purposes. Work, which includes the generation of ideas as well as the manipulation of materials, is viewed as the legitimate source of wealth.

Wealth, which can be money, reputation, self-satisfaction, honors, or whatever else of value, is important to the producer as the legitimate, accumulated profit from successful transactions in the market. This is as true of a 'poor' poet with a rich reputation among members of a comparatively small market as it is for a great merchandiser with a market of millions.

— Karl Hess[1]

---

1 Hess, Karl. *Capitalism for Kids.* Enterprise Publishing, Inc., Wilmington, DE, 1987. p. 176.

Chapter Seven
The Jobless Future

Linda Independent drives to the office as usual at 10:00 a.m. Monday morning. But in the Jobless Culture, the old definition of "usual" no longer prevails.

Ms. Independent, a morning person, has already put in three productive hours writing and directing animated InstaPrograms(™) while sipping tea in bed. Her trip to the office is one of only two she'll make this week; she and her fellow programming directors, animators, musicians, and puppeteers have agreed among themselves to meet face-to-face every Monday and Friday morning, "So we can remind ourselves we all have bodies and faces." And also so they can do some in-person project coordinating and brainstorming.

All are independent contractors who otherwise set their own hours and terms of work. Some — especially those whose creativity is stimulated by working in a group, wander in and out of the office at any hour of the day or night, using the on-site equipment, picking co-workers' brains. Others, who do better work while solitary, mostly stay home. Or sometimes even work from the beach or the mountains. It's largely up to the individual. As long as they meet their agreed-upon project obligations, how and where they do it is their own business.

No one is paid by the hour — because after all an hour measures nothing about the quality or really even the speed of the work. They're paid a negotiated fee according to what they produce. How long it takes them is entirely a matter of their own abilities and choices.

Not only is their workstyle different than in the past; so is their office. There's not a cubicle in sight. Nor an Human Resources department filled with paper-pushers. Children and dogs wander the halls. (Since the hermit types rarely come to the office, they don't have to put up with the extra noise and activity; the more social types actually enjoy it.) Office furniture consists of colorful sofas and end tables. There are even a couple of curtained cots where people putting in all-nighters can grab a quick nap.

> *No one on their deathbed ever regretted not spending more time at the office.* — Rabbi Kushner

There are bosses and managers of sorts here. And there's a company owner who ultimately contracts with all these highly independent workers. But functionally, the work hierarchies tend to be loose and flexible, with teams forming and disbanding on a per-project basis, and people taking the lead according to their natural talents or expertise in a particular area.

It's a comfortable, creative little anarchy.

"But," the early twenty-first century job-holder objects, "You've picked a bad example. Creative types have often worked in anarchic ways. Tell me how the secretaries or assembly-line grunts or bookkeepers work."

Okay ...

Well, first of all, the Jobless Culture is inherently more creative, overall, than the Job Culture ever was. So while it's entirely true that some people still work fixed hours in fixed places, even those people in rather traditional roles often have untraditional work styles. They may, for instance, work as independent contractors and set the hours they and their supervisors deem most reasonable — hours that can easily and frequently be adapted.

Rigid ideas of "full-time" and "part-time" are gone. People contract to work the number of hours, or to take on the number of obligations, that best suit them (and best suit the wide variety of companies looking for their services). Instead of being forced to fit their individual lives into a few patterns set by bureaucrats or dictated by law and regulation, people now have a rich smorgasbord of workstyle options.

A secretary whose major jobs are answering the telephone and processing documents for co-workers now might work part or even all of the day at home, with technology allowing her (or him) to transfer incoming calls to the right person and make easy changes to documents from a bedroom or kitchen table.

Bookkeepers, too, can come and go from the office — although tending to like structure more than the "creatives" do, they may opt to do their work at an office desk and keep their work separate from their homelife. But this is their decision and the decision of the businesses to which they contract their services.

The essence is choice. Not every company will offer the choices an individual wants. *Some* companies will remain extremely rigid. But there is more variety. More options.

But because no far-off bureaucracy (whether union, government, or corporate) is defining what the terms of work *must* be, people deal with each other in a vast variety of personal styles. Because there are fewer large corporations and more small businesses (as we shall see), there is much more equality between contracting parties.

But what about those assembly lines? And what about supply chains involving masses of inventory that need to be moved around the globe?

Hard work never killed anybody, but why take a chance? — Edgar Bergen

Well, for some things the old "economies of scale" rules do apply. *Some* functions are better carried out by large systems. In those cases, the need for individuals to function — part of their time — in hive-like work structures may still pertain.

But even those systems have been humanized by the wholesale cultural change that swept most of the dinosaur-bones of the Industrial Revolution's factory work-model away. Workers can more easily trade shifts with others. Thirty-hour work weeks are more common than 40, simply because of the deemphasis on the Victorian work-ethic.

And while certainly some huge corporations do cxist, it's also becoming common for those old-fashioned "economies of scale" to be achieved not solely by giant, bureaucratic institutions.

"Exploitation"

Before the Job Culture was swept away in the mid-twenty-first century, most "experts" cried that unless a myriad of fixed rules, policies, and procedures were in place to protect workers, greedy capitalists would exploit the masses. But in reality, the opposite turned out to be the case.

First off all, the vast, government-sized mega-corporations that had dominated western economies since the late nineteenth century began to come apart. The result was that most businesses became smaller, with a trend toward local ownership. Thus workers weren't so vastly dwarfed by the power of their employers. Thus, too, there were *more* companies one could work for. The result of these developments was that workers and businesses were more equal in status and negotiating power.

Entire books could be written about the factors that caused the breakup of the mega-corps. I'll mention only a pertinent few. First of all, public disgust with corporate scandals and with politicians whose votes could be bought by the biggest contributions (which nearly always came from wealthy corporations and industry groups, not from individual constituents) eventually brought a howling end to the absurd legal fiction that "corporations are persons." The notion that vast, effectively immortal, and wealthy global business interests should have "individual rights" was exposed as an absurdity. *Only individuals have individual rights.* Once that dreadful imbalance of power was addressed, the road to true equality before the law began to be built. Corporations were eventually recognized as useful business entities, but not as "persons." So their political influence plummeted — along with their ability to custom-craft legislation, make huge political contributions, and their ability to corner billions of dollars in subsidies and lopsidedly favorable government contracts.

Second, we discovered that the old "economy of scale" arguments could be seen in a different light. Very little is "economical" about a huge, inflexible institution, top-heavy with bureaucracy. In fact, modern communications and application of chaos theory led economists and business people to discover that linked chains of small, lean, innovative suppliers can deliver goods and services more efficiently than even the most highly vaunted institutional giants.

Then, lo and behold, about the time the second wave of Job Culture rebels began earning an impact in the media, everyone began to discover that much of the earlier government and union "protection" against exploitation was, in fact, a form of exploitation in itself. For instance, it finally dawned on everyone that laws and policies that defined "full-time" as 40 hours per week or "part-time" as under 25 hours per week had the effect of pounding too many square pegs miserably into round holes when limitless other possibilities were available. Also, it did no one any good to favor seniority and other non-essentials over competent work and innovation. *Even the protected employees* hadn't really benefited; they were often merely deprived of incentive, self-respect, and the joy of meeting challenges.

Because of the vast variety of other employment options available (and because the norms of the Jobless Culture simply demand more human-focused relationships), companies know they have to treat their employees and contractors well.

Still, this isn't utopia. Sometimes people are treated unfairly by those with whom they work. And sometimes, even between people of goodwill, misunderstandings or conflicting needs result in thorny problems.

With few outside parties inserting themselves into contractual relationships, private mediation and arbitration have become the norm. Instead of "solving" problems via rules, fines, or even in extreme cases prison terms imposed from above, the parties to disputes go before agreed-upon arbitrators or arbitration panels. In nearly all cases, these arbitrators bring the parties to agreement fairly rapidly and at far lower cost than under the old system of laws, regulations, and lawsuits.

In fact, employers may even offer low-cost arbitration insurance to their workers as a benefit. And independent contractors often carry arbitration policies as a matter of course.

And speaking of benefits ...

Benefits

There are, frankly, very few "job benefits" in the Jobless Culture. Independent contractors are paid well enough to fund their own vacations, sick leave, holidays, retirement plans, and insurance. But even employees have almost no "benefits" as the twentieth century understood them.

Before you say, "How horrible!" consider three things:

1. "Benefits" were always ultimately taken out of the workers' salary, anyway. If a company paid, say, $500 per month to provide health-insurance benefits for an employee, that was $500 the employee earned but didn't directly receive.
2. "Benefits" were already on their way out by the early twenty-first century, in any case, because they had become too expensive to provide. Cascading defaults on pension plans, cut-backs on health insurance, etc. had seriously weakened "benefits" (and thus seriously weakened one of the last remaining appealing features of traditional jobs) long before the Jobless Culture rose.
3. Once employees began paying for their own health care or health-insurance and controlling their own retirement funds, the costs dropped precipitously because the enormous administrative bureaucracies disappeared and because customers had incentive to shop for the most efficient and cost-effective services.

"Benefits" had only become a big part of the job picture around the time of World War II. They bound workers to certain jobs with silver chains. But ultimately, they *cost* those workers a fortune. In the Jobless Culture, workers receive more and spend it as they see fit.

They generally benefit by the elimination of "benefits."

"But who protects the people who choose not to invest for their retirement? Or who don't use their extra pay to buy health insurance?" (The voices cry from 2005 or 2010.)

You know what? That's twentieth-century thinking. The belief that some authority figure has to force millions of people to do things "for their own good" was a perfect example of elitist Job Culture thinking. Today we've discovered the obvious truth: When people know that they're solely responsible for their own well-being, they behave smarter. And those few who don't? Well, they learn that choices have consequences.

I must also add, on a positive note, that although twentieth-century style "benefits" have mostly become obsolete, independent workers have even better compensations.

Not only do they receive their *full* pay (rather than merely that part of it not handed over to administrators and bureaucrats), but most of them either own their own companies, share profits in small collaborative businesses, or otherwise negotiate extra *cash* rewards for outstanding performance.

And cash that you can use now for your own investments or pleasures beats airy, long-term promises of pensions and health care that you end up losing to corporate defaults, government regulation, inflation, or some other factor beyond your control.

Being jobless

Being jobless is no longer a social disgrace or a psychic burden. Because, after all, nearly everybody is jobless. The desire not to be a burden on others, however, has resumed its historic place. Because now if you're receiving an unemployment benefit or a welfare subsidy, you're receiving it not as an "entitlement" from some anonymous agency three thousand miles away, but more likely from the people around you. (More on the shrinking of the welfare state shortly.)

Fortunately, because the rigid 40-hour week is largely a thing of the past, there are actually more work opportunities for those who want them. Some of those opportunities are what the Job Culture might misleadingly have called "part-time." But with lower costs of many important services, less government to pay for, and (in many cases) simpler lives, "part-time" is sufficient for more and more people — as it was for their pre-industrial ancestors.

The greatest "benefit" the new system offers is the priceless benefit of *time.*

> *Doing nothing is very hard to do. You never know when you're finished.* — Leslie Nielsen

It's common for people to vary their work lives by contracting for three or four small assignments from three or four different businesses instead of precariously casting their entire life's lot in with one employer — one employer who might fail or fire them.

Small companies that had once been squeezed out by regulation and by highly subsidized competitors are thriving again. Although the media always paid much more attention to the economic impact of big businesses, in fact it was always true — and is much more true now — that small businesses generate more work for more people than big institutions do. *And* small businesses usually keep their profits within the community so everyone prospers.

There's more opportunity for those who want to contract out their services. There's more for those who want to make or do something completely independently. There's more for those in need. More for entrepreneurs. More for customers (at least in terms of personalized service and customized products). More for everybody — except far-off institutional managers and bureaucrats.

> *Those who danced were thought to be quite insane by those who couldn't hear the music.* — Angela Monet

It's not all work

But good grief — I'm making this all sound like work! Far from it. The whole point of the Jobless Revolution was to enable well-rounded lives — and that aim has largely been achieved (though not without some adjustments and unexpected consequences).

The first wave of the happily jobless tended to be highly motivated to make the life change. They swung into new activities — hobbies, homeschooling, home-based businesses, volunteer projects, neighborhood support groups, art, gardening, technological innovation, whatever — with verve and conviction.

Some — accustomed to the push-push-push of the corporate business world had a hard time learning to just take it easy. But eventually, as the culture began to shift, the media, government agencies, and even some forward-looking businesses began to tout the joys of loafing, lazing, and creative idleness. (Many of these institutional promoters of leisure, it's true, had *no* idea what a sea change they were actually wading into. They were just picking up on a trend or hoping to make money or social brownie points off of leisure advocacy.)

The first wave of the willing jobless had been seen as oddballs. But once the trend became "official," more people broke free of the job trap and even many who stayed within institutional employment began to lobby their companies for more humane concessions.

The first signs of a true Jobless Culture had begun to appear, though almost no one was really aware at the time of the enormous change just ahead.

The second wave of willing jobless contained many people who weren't as fiercely motivated as the first readers of this book. The second wave was made up of many sincere and joyful "early adopters" who'd just been waiting for such a chance. But it was also made up of others who were simply trend followers, or who wanted to work less but didn't know what they wanted to do with their free time.

These latter groups had some adjustment problems. Many of them were bored or felt they'd lost their identity once they no longer worked "full time." Some fled back to conventional jobs. Others sat around doing little or nothing, and soon became depressed. Others sought out highly scheduled "leisure" activities that weren't really very leisurely at all — from thoroughly planned-out river rafting expeditions and eco-adventures to card-playing tournaments and folk-dancing clubs.

Many of these highly structured, "other-driven" forms of leisure were big for a while. But as more and more people pulled away — psychologically, economically, and physically — from the push-push, rush-rush of the institutional business world, they also began to pull away from costly, schedule-driven, highly commercialized "leisure" activities, as well. Structured leisure, after all, had been primarily a Job Culture diversion, designed to ease the pain of structured jobs.

Similarly with electronic toys. In the first years of the Jobless Revolution, many people, young and old, submerged their newfound free time in a frenzy of video games and other digital delights. Technology continued to advance (driven largely by American creativity and offshore manufacturing) and e-toys remain a significant part of the Jobless Culture to this day.

However, after the first few years of throwing their newfound free time into an electronic frenzy, people began to lose interest. There was never any huge reassessment of the role of e-gadgets in our lives. It was simply that (as with highly organized "leisure" activities) millions gradually felt less need for ceaseless stimulation. Endless stimulation, too, had been part of the old culture, in which work and escape from work had stood as twin pillars of personal alienation and isolation. Freed from both the time constraints and the endless pressures and demands of the Job Culture, people began to calm their inner selves, crave less mindless diversion, and refocus their interests.

Sure, we still have our toys. Always will, I suppose. But we've gradually realized that the real world around us is much more interesting, and worth giving our attention to.

Soon, it became *okay* to just sit and read for an afternoon. Or to wander along a beach during what once had been the height of the work day. Or to spend time in a cafe sharing long luncheon conversations with friends. Or to take the kids on expeditions to museums in the middle of the day.

Life for most has become slower-paced and simpler once again.

And because we have time to be aware of the beauties and lures of the natural world (and because we're no long commuting or consuming as much as we once did) we've been taking better care of the environment — both the planetary environment and the parts of it that surround us in our daily lives.

Who wants to trash the world when it's more enjoyable to cultivate a planetary garden?

Another benefit: lower taxes, less government

Taxes have been dropping steadily since shortly after the Jobless Revolution began. As more and more people took up self-employment, millions discovered the real cost of taxation. When taxes had been taken out of their paychecks in weekly or biweekly increments, the amounts somehow hadn't seemed so painful. And even if the figures seemed high ...well, it's hard to truly miss money that you've never even held in your hands.

But once people had to sit down and write annual or quarterly checks to the IRS and state income tax collectors, they were horrified and began to revolt.

Some fought high taxes "within the system." Others simply shrugged and stopped paying.

Yet others, who had retained their regular jobs but decreased their number of working hours, didn't fight at all. They just lived more simply, generated less taxable income, and paid less to the bureaucrats.

And as mentioned earlier, the self-employed have many more tax deductions available to them than their conventionally employed brethren. "God bless Schedule C!" some said, as they filled out the form that enabled all those business deductions.

But the government — no surprise — began to curse Schedule C. And curse self-employment. And to step up its enforcement against those it believed had no right to call themselves independent contractors. The government was losing revenues. Losing influence. Losing power.

No one would ever say the events that followed were easy. For a time, government continued to grow, even as tax revenues fell and citizens became more fed up. State legislatures and Congress passed new taxes to make up for the shortfalls. Following the law of unintended consequences, the new taxes merely made people more angry and more willing to resist.

Congress poured billions in new funding into the IRS for tax audits, trying to stop the revolt. But much of the newly appropriated money disappeared into such bureaucratic rat-holes as the IRS's eternal (and never finished) computer upgrade. In any case, the few additional auditors who made it out onto the streets were overwhelmed by the depth of the resistance.

Since a large portion of the resistance was perfectly legal, there wasn't much the IRS or Congress could do about it anyway. People were making less money, taking a larger number of legitimate deductions, and living even better than when government statistics said they were more prosperous.

Their newfound independence made them ...well, more independent, too. People who had once simply sleepwalked through their days, too busy to worry about what the government was up to, now had time to manage their own lives better — and to learn to dislike management from above.

For a time, the government resorted to cranking up the printing presses, creating more money out of thin air to make up for the declining revenues. Ultimately, though, this proved to be a self-defeating strategy. The economic tax-spend-and-inflate house of cards, which had been growing for nearly a century, finally collapsed, as U.S. paper dollars became virtually worthless. Foreign investors stopped buying U.S. government securities. OPEC and other international organizations quit basing trade on the U.S. dollar and switched to other currencies.

There was a painful time of adjustment. But in the end, the outcome was blessed for those who value individual freedom or community self-determination.

At the end of what came to be called the Days of Downfall, government had lost its credibility. Government had shown itself to be the cause, not the solution, to major economic and social problems.

Even the most naïve no longer believed legislation, regulation, and taxation could solve every inequity or injustice. The government's desperate attempt to keep itself afloat with vast influxes of unbacked paper currency had literally robbed people of their savings and their other assets — and laid bare the old lie that "the government is your friend." Now nearly all of us realized that government is, at bottom, both a thief and a bully.

People becoming accustomed to independence in their work and family lives also began to realize that real solutions to real problems begin (and usually also end) closer to home. For the first time in history, government agencies actually began to disband, lay off their workers, and even sell off their buildings and other assets.

During the Days of Downfall, millions who depended on government jobs, subsidies, and other largess definitely suffered. Doomsayers predicted starvation in the streets.

But then a strange thing happened.

The young climate of entrepreneurship and independence that had been growing before the Downfall exploded into new life. With central governments actually shrinking and bureaucrats losing their jobs, and with companies contracting with suppliers and workers on a wide variety of customized terms, there was suddenly more work for anybody who wanted it and was able to do it.

Money generated wasn't sent off to distant agencies, where bureaucrats were paid to do nothing productive. Money went toward products and services real people valued. It went toward growing healthy businesses and communities.

The world that emerged was hardly perfect. No society ever is. But the few who were both unable to work and had no support from family, soon found help within the community. Funny thing; individuals in neighborhoods, churches, and communities have always been best at spotting those who genuinely need help. And with the vast, resource-sucking federal and state welfare bureaucracies no longer absorbing three dollars out of every four supposedly earmarked for the unfortunate, the real unfortunate were able to get local help.

If anyone starved in the streets, no one ever heard about it. Somehow, even former third-assistant middle-managers from the Department of Redundancy Department quickly discovered useful skills and a willingness to use them. Or (because families no longer needed two wage-earners), they settled down to become stay-at-home parents and discovered a new old way of living. Those who genuinely couldn't work found support from a variety of churches and charities — now far better funded, since contributors weren't having such a large percentage of their income milked in advance by government.

Although foreign investors now shunned government securities and U.S. paper currency, they were attracted by the tremendous energy and innovation that exploded outward as government imploded. Foreign money spurred the re-birth of the U.S. economy. But domestic investment with the new metal-backed U.S. dollar soon eclipsed it.

Although Jefferson and Madison would hardly have recognized the innovative, technologically vibrant world of the late twenty-first century, they would certainly recognize the spirit of its people:

> The class of citizens, who provide at once their own food and their own raiment, may be viewed as the most truly independent and happy. They are more: They are the best basis of public liberty, and the strongest bulwark of public safety. It follows, that the greater the proportion of this class to the whole society, the more free, the more independent, and the more happy must be the society itself.

This is just one possible (and sketchy) view of what a Jobless Culture might look like. No mere writer gazing forward from the perspective of the early twenty-first century can really know. Neither can any "expert," even if he gives himself the grand title "futurist."

But however it looks, a world in which people have a great deal more freedom and latitude to balance their work with the rest of their lives is well worth looking forward to.

Chapter Eight
Getting There

Getting to a true Jobless Culture is not going to be easy. Or fast. To anybody who's anxious to push such a culture into being, the most useful thing I can say is *relax*. Encourage cultural change to happen naturally, and in the meantime, enjoy both your own growing satisfactions and the joy of spreading the meme.

The Jobless Culture must either emerge from individuals' true desire for a different life or not emerge at all.

In many of us idealists, the urge to save the world is strong. The only problem is that (if we're very honest with ourselves) one of the biggest things the world needs to be saved from is people who want to save the world.

Too often, we try to *impose* whatever we believe to be a good idea — never mind that others might disagree with us, or might simply not be ready to go our way.

Genuine healthy cultural change should never — and actually *can* never — be imposed from above, whether through legislation, regulation, or dictatorial fiat.

Imposed change can succeed for a while and can certainly give politicians or corporate executives something to brag about. But imposed change always ends up creating stresses and cracks that eventually lead to everything from grumbling discontentment to outright revolution.

So we must resist the urge to push any new culture into being. If it helps, let's recognize that our urge to use force (e.g. laws or regulations) to impose change on others is, in itself, a manifestation of the style of thinking that leads to both police states and highly institutionalized Job Cultures.

Genuine cultural change is slower, but healthier and longer-lasting.

So that's what we should aim for.

Now *how?*

> *It is foolish to postpone enjoyment of your ordinary life until you are more successful, more secure, or more loved than you are today.* — Timothy Ray Miller

Making the change

- First, we should endeavor to live our own lives in as much balance as we can. Even if we must be *in* the Job Culture, we do not have to be *of* it.
- Start the sort of business you'd like to work for, with humane working conditions, flexible hours, and (to whatever extent the IRS will "allow" it) independent workers. Even if most such businesses end up staying small, we're still changing the world one company at a time. Such businesses also teach by example how the Job Culture can change.
- Teach your children about the joys of independent, self-chosen work. If you can take them out of government school and encourage them to learn through hands-on creativity, making, doing, and exploring things for themselves, all the better.

- Take the opportunity to teach others in your community who want to know how they, too, can escape the job trap and minimize the impact of the Job Culture. This teaching might take the form of one-on-one conversations, community workshops (for employers or employees), demonstration projects in community technology, or simply something as pleasant and beneficial as getting your business featured in a local newspaper article.
- As much as possible, patronize businesses that reflect your ideals. This may mean very different things to each of us. But in general, if given a choice between Wal-Mart and a well-run local store selling similar merchandise, go local. If given a choice between buying a new General Motors product or an alternative means of transportation, go with the used vehicle or the recumbent trike.
- Let businesses know why you're patronizing them — or why you're not. Tell your friends and neighbors, too. Even if at first they have no interest in the kind of change you're promoting, or even if at first they don't see the point of choosing businesses based on human and humane considerations, you'll have done something important. You'll have planted the meme. Someone who's uncomprehending today may have an "Aha!" experience based on your ideas tomorrow.

Vision is where tomorrow begins, for it expresses what you and others who share the vision will be working hard to create. Since most people don't take the time to think systematically about the future, those who do, and who base their strategies and actions on their visions, have inordinate power to shape the future. — Burt Nanus

- Start or participate in online forums that focus on simple living, independent business, community-building, frugality, or whatever topics you believe would best help you stay your own course and encourage others to overcome the difficulties of remaining independent in a world of passivity and dependency.
- Start an organization to encourage or publicize the virtues of the balanced, job-free life.

Starting an organization has both virtues and drawbacks. Organizations can be effective at bringing in and encouraging fledgling independents. Simply by issuing news releases, they can often get an amount of publicity for a cause that far outstrips the organizations' actual size and importance. But organizations tend quickly to become another form of institutional establishment. And people within "do-gooding" organizations too often automatically turn to coercive, usually governmental, solutions (e.g. lobbying for laws that would *force* businesses to offer more flexibility to workers).

The Job Culture was imposed through political and economic coercion. (Or rather, the pre-conditions for it were imposed for the benefit of mass production; we then fleshed in the details ourselves by filling our exhausted off-hours with TV watching, fast-food gobbling, mall-shopping, and sitting in traffic.) Therefore, the Job Culture has always rested uneasily on human beings — especially on those of us who perceive potential for other ways of life. If we make the mistake of *imposing* what we believe to be superior, we'll only repeat the same kind of historic mistake.

> *Mastering others requires force; Mastering the self requires enlightenment.*
>
> *He who conquers others is strong, he who conquers himself is mighty.* — Lao Tzu

It may be, in the best possible case, that once a moderate-sized jobless movement takes hold, it will become harder for anyone to impose vast systems of rules on others — whether those rules are of the old Job Culture or wrong-headed attempts to impose the Jobless Culture.

Institutions are breaking down already, even if we can't yet see them cracking and crumbling. Their ability to impose anything is weakening, even as their attempts to impose are ramping up.

The governments of the western world have become top-heavy in their command-and-control mentality. At the moment, they seem enormously powerful — and they are in the process of expanding and consolidating their control. Modern governments seem to believe there is simply no area of human endeavor that they can't monitor, finance, or otherwise control.

But this power growth is in part an illusion. Expanding power over others isn't a sign of strength; it's a sign of weakness and fear.

"We the People" may no longer have much direct say over a government whose daily workings are largely the result of the decisions of career bureaucrats — a government where few of us are actually represented by our "representatives." But governments are still sustained by three things: our money, our dependence on their services, and our belief that government can be an all-powerful solution to all problems. If we withdraw these three things — or even substantially weaken any of those three supports, government ultimately has far less power to impose anything on anyone.

I realize that weaker government is a happy prospect for libertarians, and perhaps a frightening prospect for some others. But if we're looking to free ourselves from the Job Culture and from servitude to the industrial or post-industrial machine, then all of us should wish to move away from society's top-down command-and-control structures.

Similarly, but on a smaller scale, the mega-corporations of the world may be weakening just when it looks as if they're going to take over the globe. First of all, many of them rely heavily on government subsidies, contracts, and policies, as we've seen. When governments weaken, so do the giant corporations they've helped build and maintain. Also *if* there's even a modest movement toward a Jobless Culture, that, too, will weaken giant global business structures. Finally, the unpredictable workings of the universe simply don't favor any large institution in the long run. Bureaucracy and top-down control may rule the day, but the centuries are ruled by change — something large institutions aren't very good at.

The more we are able to earn our livings in independent, self-directed ways ...the more time we have to think and act for ourselves ... the more we and our community rely on each other for the sustenance of life ... then the less we need far-off benefactors — who we must remember are also far-off bosses. Sometimes very arbitrary and savage ones.

The less we need far-off bosses, be they in bureaucracies or boardrooms, the more we — and all those around us — will own our own lives.